bill bissett

th book

talonbooks

Talonbooks
278 East First Avenue, Vancouver, British Columbia, Canada V5T 1A6
www.talonbooks.com

First printing: 2016

Typeset in Helvetica Neue
Printed and bound in Canada on 100% post-consumer recycled paper

Cover design by Jordan Stone
Front cover photograph courtesy of Rose-Marie Tremblay
Back cover photograph courtesy of Mark Belvedere

Talonbooks gratefully acknowledges the financial support of the Canada Council for the Arts, the Government of Canada through the Canada Book Fund, and the Province of British Columbia through the British Columbia Arts Council and the Book Publishing Tax Credit.

Library and Archives Canada Cataloguing in Publication

Bissett, Bill, 1939–, author
        Th book / bill bissett.

Poems written in the author's own phonetic language.
ISBN 978-0-88922-980-8 (paperback)

        I. Title.

PS8503.I78B66 2016   C811'.54   C2015-908294-3

"We are larger for our loving despite th trembling
of our hearts…" – Helen Posno

"…i got th book inside my hed…" p 70 peter among
th towring boxes   talonbooks

4 penny east n cayle chernin n jackie burroughs n
david melville n lenore coutts n hannalore hedley
n dennis johnson n p.k. page n elizabeth brewster
n michelle bissett n mitzi kerwin n robert kroetsch
n cory monteith n maury chakin n doug randle n
frankie rich n edna randle n robert sutherland n
valerie lapointe n mavis gallant n anne hebert
n karen preisler n jacqueline juriansz
…n sean kirwin n jamie reid
manee othrs   all such brite lites 4 art   brillyant
mirrors n opnings 2 us all evree step uv th way

sum uv thees pomes apeerd previouslee in
arc vallum 4 poets rampike
thanks 2 carin makuz 4 th littr pome prompt
thanks agen 2 workman arts n th secret
handshake toronto & 2 jordan stone my life
coach & 2 th ontario arts council 4 a grant
2 go deepr in2 n develop mor n compleet
ths work   yo yo meow is my mothrs cat
& thanks 2 her as well n 2 bertrand lachance
thanks 2 miles benton 4 th titul th brain in
th glass jar n 2 linda rogers van krugel n
rick van krugel who stood by n
helpd me n my dottr 4 manee yeers

as if   almost embarasing
2 b

cum upon looking
4 images among th leevs n
mulch in th courtyard th
moon liting up onlee sum uv
th possibul cache in th seeming
infinit darkness   i will not give
yu what yu want th vois sd 2 me
thees ar not gud 4 yu n yu will
onlee find distans n dissatis
facksyun ther   i will give yu
words n images   that sum
times evn with th mould
compost smells   sumtimes
sing

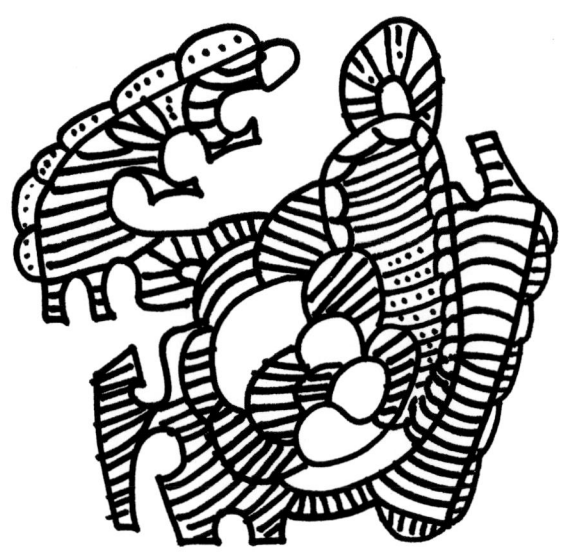

place

places 2 let placelets places uv th heart yu
alwayze have a   places uv consciousness
places wher iuv livd wun place i nevr wantid
2 leev waitid ther 4 thirtee yeers off n on 4
sum wun 2 arriv 2 cum n what happend n
did not happn lace ace my love uv naytur
                         pl url
                    place uv dreems wher
                  yu put things i put it ther
               no thats not th place ium
                waiting 4 my place ment   tryin
            2 find my home place place mats ar
                thees th wuns yu reelee liked
                   i want 2 place my heart
                 in yr hand first i gotta take it
                 out
                 my heart   air it out see
                    whos put ther   wher
                 voyage 2 th inside uv th heart
              wher its place reelee is
            whers yr place i lost my
              place in th first place
                 sew he tuk him 2 his
                 place n thats wher
                 he lost his place
                    wher

enial d i denial

th tree uv lite s life

dew yu want 2 b on it

in it in on it calm

with it within it

processyuns changing erth projekt

o u i o u o

hungree throat eeting breething
lake on th mountain th brain is
hungree 2 n just whn we thot th
narrativ epoch was ovr   see th pro
cessyuns   ooooouuuuuuuuuuuuuuuuu
uuuuuuuuuuuu lettr texting letting go
th oooooooooooooooo ride
bingul uuuuuuuuuuuuuuuu bangul
th awakening ar we still on 4
wednesday   th inventivness uv th
mind   th rind uv demons n moon
soakd lustr   wher is evreething
actualitee   dripping in2 us

whn my fathr n dottr first met
in hevn

they complaind abt me
aftr telling each othr how much
   they admired each othr

   they set in on mor griping abt me

   fathr sd he was nevr th son i wantid
   no lawyr ther sum kind uv ballet
   boy i worreed sew 4 his securitee
   i had 2 cut him out uv my will

   i undrstand my dottr sd he cudint
      control things n th
   situaysyuns around us veree well
   n nevr ernd enuff 4 us why oh why
   did he want 2 b an artist

   tho 4 a long time in latr yeers   he
   did help me a lot with munee n food
     n veree consistentlee my dottr sd
   almost proudlee

may b he did alrite my fathr sd oh yes
my dottr sd he bcame 2 dew alrite
         oh i miss him my dottr
sd sew dew i my fathr sd n they
   both wer veree sad with missing me

he reelee was veree sweet my dottr sd
n hard working 2   my fathr sd yu cant
  xpekt
      artists 2 dew as well as lawyrs no my
      dottr sd n they both cried at th same
            time we reelee miss him

      me i woke up skreeming

dere great empress ths needs work

th loop hole in my
current transmisyun 2 yu tho is whn i slip in
abt my prsonal life being elusiv 2 me

what is that i know its a code 4 gettin it
on with sumwun with all thats bin going on
th shock n sumtimes derangement n th
reassuring work iuv bin missing that th
gettin it on with sumwun starting 2 its bin
ovr a month

whats up with me thinking thats sew
prsonal   like evreething it is n it isint yes
th work is ok thats what reassuring meens
prsonal th greef is prsonal sew is a pome
going ok wher it wants 2 n kleening n buro
kratik work   thats all prsonal if yu put yr
heart in2 it n how els 2 dew

yes sew th gettin it on   bodeez flyin in
th air n on th bed   chair floor   th flin
flon arabesque   n th comfort uv sumwun ther
being ther   iul pay attensyun 2 that whn
i can   what can yu dew ium telling myself

dont not 2 evn whn sumwun goes 2 spirit
    yu love n its all ium thinkin abt
aftr a time a whil lose faith in it th find
  ing uv anee prsonal love loving th
    othr prsons bodee around yu yrs a
round his hers dont loos faith in it   just
    bcoz thrs no futur   in making love
gettin it on   n it sew   changes evn
    leevs yu
              evreething duz

memoree

is ther identitee without
memoree yes that wud
b identitee without memoree
sum peopul call soul

xcellent n th word identitee
starts we notis with an "i"
n whats th deel ther with dent
teeth a serious but not life
thretening accident

thats all i can say 4 now

xsept même is th french
word 4 same   sew that konstrukt
hi lites that matching n sort
ing counting ar th bases uv
civilizaysyuns

4 trade warehousing n a basis uv
logik 4 a lot uv our thinking n sew
memoree wud b rowing 2 th
same is it or eeeeee shhh

orrrrr cest sa fate is oftn ironik
sew is memoree
with th filing n th storage mor me
all wayze   mor me thats yu mor
or is it   eeeeeeee

remembr aftr th shock n rebuild
ing yr mind from th ground up th
gud memoreez can help yu thru

th reptilian fold   is not evreething

moonlite nite   a curv in th sky
yu cud swing on hot fireworks
fireworks ovr th vallee he cums
4 yu inside th rooms uv th college
late at nite   yu get it on 4 th first
time n sew far nevr 4get

th first time n yu store thos
images   hands touch his swetr
fingrs mouths n arms around yu
n th storee   th oree in storee
n memoree how we reakt 2 how
we hold n file th images uv th next

xperiens hold th memoree wch

evreewun duz diffrentlee is how
n why as its   changing passing
  thru

  th storee

aumoeer

2 cum in

mu reeo

umaiaou

meergao

leevaunsi

a goldn willow tree n me wer
sighing sighing sighing sighing ing ing
not sew free not sew free n
me mooving 4ward with
my limitid mind mind mind mind

reemago um mu go ag rag ro

goo agomeer mu um og gar

or oga remko my name is she

sighd ramer reef sels om

kuom winko kemro marer efer

komusid kinwo tendr bulbous

pull th boat in at th noat hou n

th trengul arbora danguls 4 all 2

seed tempestuous night weer

scalds th eye lids barking at th

bay windows th estrn nitengail

dreems uv yu n me n th lardr ro

bins wungs swillows darkest d

angr alludes 2 th elysium sank

shuaree o deer robetr tree aro

usinf angyls N GULS u u u ths

n that trembuls my arms arou
nd yu lees th weesuls yj not ev
ents un events eaguls crows
ravens swallows cardinal s wood
peckrs vulshurs sprawling ovr th
roof tops crowns uv mercuree an
nounsrs uv cumming   changes
glandular delusyuns or illusyuns
u mite call it th dogs barking th
rousing shreeks uv feer in th
all nite   th bats fly   inn
we stoppd ther 4 a whil n
suppd on sum lettus n sweet t
was it th wind or reelee my
mind mind mind mind mind
mi im d n din dim mid callo
th wrenching mim seqwestr
us n th remonstrans
zero in flite mind
th lardr ceiling
us n th rubee
repreev

whats   nu

a rivr uv gold
is flowing thru
all our   hearts

aabbbbbbbb

uuUUOoommm

wwwWeeeeeee

scape scope 2

xxXxxxxxXXXXxu_{uu}aru

soonloo**om**muarshescuyu

ehnoonmoom**moom**dontruvu

vuyuahnoonmomoo**md**oon

truvuyu**he**

didyu**Su**gg**estyth**tre**mo**rr**

edhsiteuv th dockyads b4thais

seewashdinovr al theyr houses

asbonkeeasnothingleftbereftc

ud **b**

we lern 2 love th fleeting

thats it th fleeting th changing is th flickring
th auras cascading in2 mor changing wher is
th organ permanens th permanent embrace
projekt

maybe thr is no leeving onlee changing th
allwayze turning n running 2 cum cum n go
b n leev evn as if n thr is no leeving sure
yu say thats going 2 far well evn th invisibul
realm can respond 2 us

it sure is far 4 sirtin farthr thn our hearts go
sumtimez each not alwayze in inside th fethrs
n vessels n th rivrs running blood n evreething
els sing n th song shifts lokaysyun yes th
pain uv not seeing her

almost a yeer latr my dottr is speeking 2 me
oftn me feeling sew morose n my whol being
bleek n hurting   daddee its alrite   its ok ium
ok me i dont let myself get it on a common
greef stratajee self denial selabesee as if that
wud bring her back sumhow help tho 4 a long
time it duz help 2 not prsonalee love sum wun

2 deny myself my pleysyurs 2 b alert 2 her may
be cuming back   2 keep vigil 4 her returning

how long ar we evr in th present if evreething
bcums a memoree live in memoree chanting
til th past alwayze within us tho not as in bag
gage letting go uv that tho thats alredee all
wayze heer redee 2 pack waiting on th cor
onrs report they nevr satisfy 4get i calld sum
wun will call back they nevr dew

realitee in th leed metaphysiks alwayse run
ning a close second heer 2day gone 2morro
tho nevr reelee gone   gone onlee inside an
othr realm   dew yu feel releesd from th pains
uv erthling worreez loss hurts darling   eye
askd daddee dont worree   its not like that   yu
can b alrite ium not getting ovr ths passing
we change th greef changes us what dew we
reelee know realm 2 realm we connekt enjoy
each day sure uv what ther is no answr

th pathwayze 2 wher we ar konnekting erth
wayze art bizness opnings hopes n th travel
ling th tactilitee grace how we can live in
th image lettrs thrill uv writing each lettr hold
ing shaping offring th pickshur images breth

breething heer 2 b heer until   we ar not   n
we r sum wher els byond th lites n shadows
th mercuree tangents th rush n wundrful
fulfillments how long th wind was last nite
n th almost seizures in th bath tub   b4 th
phone call from th hospital far away n wher
iud just bin how tiny kreetshurs we all ar
n our ideas sew big 2 huge like our heds
    4 our bodeez n we fly thru taxis rain sky
    sunshine running   running 2 see her b
    with her

planes teers n we fly n hang with each othr
in th hospital 4 hours 4evr until all uv th soul
goez n she flies away sew far away whn i cud
alwayze find her no mattr how she was hiding
sum times it tuk months   n now we had a reel
ee gud routeen freqwent n reliabul evreething
n she is evn sew far away now inside my hed n
heart as

alwayze whnevr she wants thats th magik
greef nevr letting go n whnevr eye want
nevr letting go n thru endless teers choking
n stumbuling with th word want sew changes

sew much help from frends th empress diana
phoning me in th cab 4 her n 4 shane letting
go letting go n ther is no go whnevr it plays
well shes always heer like th stars n th god
dess wind on th lake

on th mountain outside uv trenton wher mo
hawk peopul livd n also came 4 heeling
ceremoneez from montréal or hochelaga as
it was previouslee calld shes alwayze heer
n wher she is   our dottr sew lovd by us n
by sew manee   she is dansing in th stars now
n th brite breething skiez my dottr is jordan
counseling me on th cell in th taxi th airport
th hospital yr dottr is brain ded now th doktor
held me its unlikelee she will revive

n th wind goddess dansing above th lake on
th mountain   my dottr michelles organs
taking healthee hold in nu peopul she dusint
need thos aneemor wher she is flying thru
th milkee wayze n othr magik places all chang
ing within infinit changing my dottr is free
uv all physical bonds limits burdns wher she
is going thr is such singing n play we heer
within erth bounds can onlee dreem uv n th

love we feel 4 th fleeting thats wher we can
love   no holding jordan n othr frends adeena
roger david dr paula phoning me in th taxi 2
th airport leeving toronto theyr calls helping
me deep breething crying skreeming running
2 th plane they say ium 2 late 4   thrs emptee
seets on it ium running running crying my
dottr needs me 2 get on 2 see her th amay
zing air canada prson sz if we run n get ther b
4 th door closes yu can get on sit aneewher
fast fastr   1 second b4 th door closes ium in
n sitting   staring 5 hours in2 space 4 th lite
uv my dottr   each moment each beet n
changing dwindling she odeed on cocaine a
veree low grade uv cocaine th doktor sd what
happend sew fast she had bin kleen n sobr 4
three yeers she was starting 2 write wundrful
poetree i had just bin ther n had just talkd with
her a few dayze ago n she had left me a
message that evreething was ok evreething
changes sumtimes i we cudint find her she
was living outside but now she had xcellent apt

n as thats wher we reelee ar living th changing
we lern 2 love howevr reluctantlee sorrow
greef we maybe dont evr reelee get ovr dr lisa
ms lasalle mr pete phoning me in th comfort inn

victoria   kathy n bill sheffeld arriving her
othr parents n my mothrs joy n jena n
princess rosa n betsy n michelles son
dalton n orville michelles partnr all uv
us gathring with each othr 2 see thru th
arrangements moma joy dewing it all n
th greef n th witnessing that bcum parts
uv us n accept th fleeting whn duz that
happn th acceptans   onlee sumtimez

a yeer n a half latr i feel like sum wun
who has bin sick 4 a long time didint
know it n is onlee now cumming back
or not a yeer n a half latr i get it on with
sum wun at last i may b getting thru sum
uv th first stages uv greef finding my own
life i dont sumtimez want enuff

wun place i was in th place uv endless scald
ing teers wher bilyuns uv peopul go 2 let go
th howling skreeming loss until we can bcum
mor grayshus accepting life deth changes
whn it cums n goez th place seems alwayze
ther   programmd in us now n sew neer th
surface what redee at anee time 2 leep on
us th loss   i can onlee sum timez bare

sumtimes i want evreething

thn i realize i alredee have evreething
or what is ther 2 have no thats not rite

sumtimez i think evreething is on its way

no thats not rite

awsum maybe thats how it is how is it
what is evreething how can we find it

is it inside us no but that seems rite

its 4 sure not outside us

or is it have yu seen evreething latelee
have i can that happn what is evreething
can yu talk with it evreething is on th
event horizon or is it th event nd th
horizon yu can ride on it sleep with it
thats a gud part take out take in away its
all ther 4 yu evreething is that rite i dont
know if i get that ium alredee inside
evreething evreething is inside me
indivisibul nd a part a change uv see

th journee 2 hevin

wuns undrway is veree smooth sailing
rescue circuls ar all ovr th world
n help peopul thru   who cant beleev n
accept they ar what erthlings call ded n
ar freeking n self tormenting abt theyr
own loss
uv life

psychiks in rescue circuls evreewher
help th erth borne spirits in2 theyr next x
perienses if yuv seen th othrs with
nicole kidman thn yu know ths is what
can happn a veree poignant n brillyant
depicksyun uv th innr trubbuls that can
4ground

sew first we leev th bodee not always
sew grayshuslee n thn we ar tho ultima
atelee as in latr on a bit we look sereen
as if wev seen sumthing sew beautiful
we feel wundr n awe n relaxaysyun

n thn we ar takn 2 deepreckling dee
breething at last tho all parts uv it dee
breefing   place cell leevustransfr
place withinbrushing past th realm uv
sighs not visibul from aneewher els

i loaflid past gingerarilee in a shovulwrappd
enklowshjur yar no tingus now shutting off th
neon textyuralis th sympotolojees uv taste
shuffulin off th mortal coilage no air

2 th brainwear all th switches shutting
off wun at a time   sumtimes multi fasiting
wind downings   all th mouth uv breeth
ing nevr th last wun   inside thees hallwayze
wrappd in side a red crimson tube thats
th next th red crimson tube   pulsing
pulsing valving   vulving ving rheeeaa
red crimson   all th sunlite enshrounding
th textual digital carpeting heer not a

sound evn 2 brek   or interrupting ths
smoothest uv all   delivree systems nevr
stopping how oftn dew peopul go 2 spirit
places   in th red crimson tube   all th
bad memoreez ar drained out like bad
blood   n run thru tubes   from th bodee

in2 garbage   bad memoreez gone
onlee gud   memoreez   remaining   2 go

sew its easier 2 leev erth 2 leev th place
s uv transisyun n proseed on 2 th levls
dimensyuns realms wher bad memoreez
ar unknown unknowabul unknown n
un knowing

ths processing all takes what we on erth
call time we lay ther in th crimson
tube 4 what we on erth wud call weeks or
what we also call sleep th crimson tube

hums n shakes a littul   sum bad memoreez
ar hard 2 drain th ride can b bumpee cumming
out uv theyr storage areas in th brain n tissus
n in th aurik memoreez dropping them dissolv

n all th gud memoreez cum up we keep them
theyr a keepr   thees glandular tissued brain
chemical based aurik info all erth bound sew
attachments ar drawn out uv us all ths

deebreefing takes a whil th proselediters pro
seedyur can varree   duz in fakt varree from
prson 2 prson going in2 his or her red
crimson tube thr is no wun size fits all

n gradualee sew gradualee inkreementalee
2 th spirit place s wher th total emphasis is

on heer not wher sew much is wher heer
is at ths moment wher is heer or ther
no
is heer yes references 2 wher b is in
onlee
shadows grayzing heeling glaysing all
th present hevinlee fields minding
unminding
spheer
realm

atmospheer
dimensyun

its   molekular   all th   way

dissolv   dissolving

whn he first walkd in2 th bar

i saw problem writtn all ovr him
his aura seemd sew paind n distraut
he sat down n sd 2 me her unfair
angr at me at first cawsd me a
painful urinaree infeksyun i thot
n i was reelee passing stones is
that letting go   sew ium letting it
go like stones cumming out uv my
cock wun stone at a time   n uv
kours sumtimes mor

if we kling

2 what we think is our
identitee thn we cannot
change if we cannot change
we cant live   th mind is a
kaleidoscope   it needs 2 turn
on a dime byond our
2 visceral responses   our
reptilian fold strikt prmissyuns
we need 2 xperiens change
thats what life is   see evree
thing with nu eyez evree day
n nite   take less offens no
mor battuls sabotage no
mor killing   love our
changing selvs   roles
dynamiks   letting go
no didaktik no censor no
oppressyun dominans uv
self   ther ar sew manee choices
with art   without art   without yu
without me   with yu   with me yu

ar not onlee wher yu ar   yu
ar part uv yr alwayze travelling
      home carrees n uncarreez
      with yu me us   each
         buttrfly n mountain n
            drum beet go th rivr
         we ar in is alwayze
         changing th fluiditee
            uv our dreems
               n lives   sum
            times i reelee undr
            stand standing undr
         sumtimes i need help
            th meditaysyun soothes
      th struggul   n th changing
         continues   a star in our
            hand n our swimming
               eyez in th moon   sail
         ing thru our dansing wayze
didint yu heer that sound in
         th mountain blessing yr
            tendr dayze n time

th fate uv bugs on a windshield

is harsh what if thats yu   dew
yu worree abt bugs on a wind
shield   n what happns 2 them
wud yu want 2 b wun uv them

reinkarnaysyun bluez   help

thos bugs on a windshield
mite have a soul 2   help   help

aftr th show th beautee uv that moment

i hope iul remembr 4 a long time   how
aftr th consert outside on granville st
    evning sew on
we spontaneouslee startid dansing 2
    that song from th triplets uv belleville
a bit creole   a bit django a bit ska   th
    singrs wer playing inside that song n
    no linguistik msundrstanding or unpro
vokd angr at me that happend latr   can
        evr take that away   that moment
uv us sew heartfelt n brillyantlee dansing
    reelee with each othr on rue granville
aftr th show n tell   n how can yu tell n
    tell me   what   was her tell that next
day   raining sew hard   i didint see
    cumming

37

th storee uv all ok most relaysyunships

yr not turning out th way i wantid

peeling kiwi at sun set

 i think ium dewing ok
ium not disturbing
th platelets n th

hyeena n buzzards
ar still sum distans
away

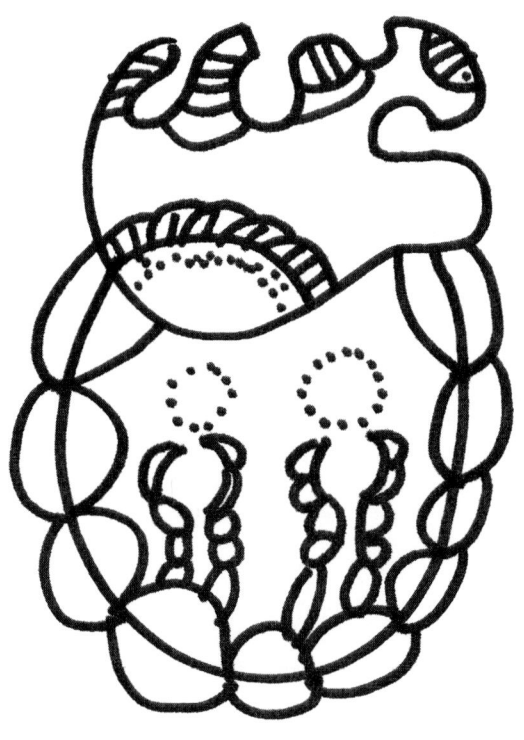

anna n andrew vegetaybuls

wuns agen wer dansing sew fine
in th lokal ice rink nowun
will give yu a back rub 4 as long
as yu want 2 along th gold
route n th fast licorice trail
they felt n not 4 th first time
how they relied n wud still
gain strength from they wer
going 2ward dog kreek ther
was a suddn tip tapping at th
door n it was th pack rat
wanting 2 get in n th raven sd
nevr mor as i am up all nite
translating mary shelleys
frankenstein oh isint it
alredee in english i askd
well th prson sd dr raven he
was licensd 2 neuromansee
mooving it in2 th langwage
uv 2day   ahh i sd th langwage
uv 2day a line rememberd
whn at last they wer happee
wud they like it thers alwayze

a gap 2 fill sailors in th theatre
maybe life is in th slippage hes
taut me a lot uv things she sd
n th railway running thru all our
heds n th pillow peopul sew
wunderd is it time 2 leev th
hotel yet

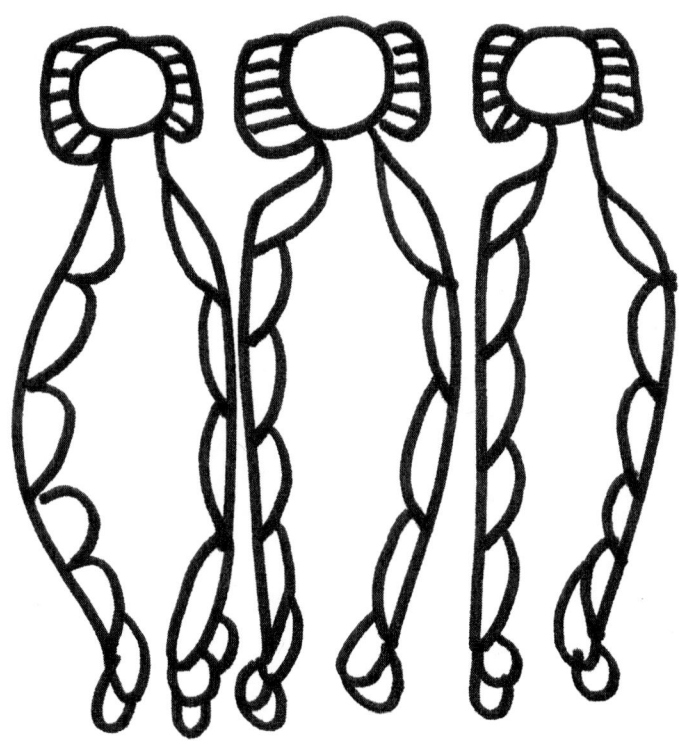

we ar almost ther

yu can find
　　　aneething uv
aneething
　　　　aneewher
at anee time

th ride

    dont figur nothing
dont figur nothing
is evreething relaysyunal n kontextual
isint evreething relaysyunal n kontextual
  i walkd 2 th end uv th pier
                waiting 4 a lift off watr taxi
     air float flat was th feeling despair was
   my hous not that cud not b get 2
  gethr with sum wun it dusint mattr who
    sum wun is on his or her way i saw a
   sparkling lite drawing neer no
       guilt no shame no longing
     its heer now its heer now nothing 2
  figur nothing 2 undrstand th wait
   4 th lift off was sew worth it
    th silvr pier   th air watr float
     opns its wings 2 me i go
      inside th ride is starting
       dont need 2 hold on
       dont need 2 let go

sew i askd jeffrey

what duz aneething
meen n he sd anee
thing meens what
evr yu want it 2
sew aneething meens
evreething it can

can we reelee lern th
reel trewth storee uv what
it is   that jeffrey sd   oh
can we   reelee admit th
flexibilitee   uv our minds
th multiplisiteez opsyuns

speeking loudr thn words
we have n make sew
much stuff n th detail
th illusyuns as it sew
oftn is ar   peopul made
man/woman made
evree brain is diffrent
n prson made n inheritid
th perplexitee 2ward n th
nuans accent n approach 2

rivrs uv neglekt surfeit uv
unsirtintee n rapturous
knowing whn we cum 2 th
abyss we ar alredee in n
falling falling tremors uv
manee realms uv consciousnes
embrace touching n care
surroundid by delusyuns uv
delusyuns letting thos doomd
narrativs flow thru n around
us n being wher we ar
as if thats sew eezee ther
accept th embrace uv th
infinit unsirtinteez   hard 2
dew n worth it   it is sd th
great creator gives us all at
leest wun gift wch focus lens
n how equalitee can inkrees
a surprize phone call   i love
th pam familee   a constant
low hiway hum i cudint live
ther   eye think thats 45 laps
almost drowning in a see uv
narrativs negativ n who can
eet them all frazzuld whippd by
template town ths life is sew strange
n is nevr not strange

now that we r in hevin

alwayze remembr
god is a lot uv fun n
hes shes its sorree 4 all th
shit we have 2 go thru
heer on erth   2 have
a gud life but its not his
her its fawlt   god cudint
help it   xsept 4 our g-d n
goddesses allah inside us
sew manee names 4 we wear
stars n hevins n glooskap
breethd life in2 each wun uv us
aftr skulpting us from eastern
atlantik clay dna its almost all
up 2 us   th key is almost

we have th choices th
choices have us by th
in th can yu find
climb th stares th odds
chances evreething
changes evreething
evn god th evree thing
we live inside   balls n
cross hairs

i live in a well

its parshulee
pollutid

ths is a deep
image
pome

sumtimez i
remembr
evreething

sumtimez i
remembr
nothing

whats th diffrens

can yu tell

dew yu know

young mastrs uv pinto

watchful th climb
in2 orange peel
layd on th rite side
th hung gardn th way
1/2 way up or down
th cliff

a rush uv leevs
thru th partlee opend
curtain
touches th window

wher th watr goez
aftr my bath
aftr drinking
and th tap is turnd off

we wash th window
2 bettr feel th moon
thru it

apertures thees ar

uv th mind its hanging gardns
we thred thru
   its own needul eye

discloses alwayze

form on form

  in our orange room
painting hung
  a struggul
1/2 way up or down
  a cliff anee uv them

and no lie

  life as an infinit
   mental note
hastilee ascribed
  2 th othr

  NO
its me   heer now
  writing ths pome
not knowing deth
  we derive form
   from

ium going 2 sleep soon
in my purpul haven my lids shut
  on othr opnings

life aftr deth b4 nd aftr

sew he she is ded
  and now we can know
thees things
  that it is th ded
we thrive on
  that lulls us ourselvs
in2 ghost wrapprs

 form form from is form
   foam teeth and deth ar form
   formd by form they cum gnashing
   theyr feetshurs formd alwayze lost
    in form informd farming it is th
   wind framing
     and a green sigh image arming
console ourselvs us alwayze happns
  ths mort   morf form

deth as melodee 2 love form

life is deth 2 firm love form circular
life dulld 2 adore equals is ar we

felt alive thn that time and thn r
n now kreetshur 2 myself   deth

will still b a surprise   or not n

listning 2 th watr fall ovr th train
staysyun n all its epik industrial

bleekness   we see traces uv ourselvs
in drawings   erasing disapeering in
th watr n rust   heer alwayze opning 2
othr worlds   let us in   let us in all th
        way in   yes is i a joke   or an
  evolushyunaree plateau n thrust

pleez whil thers time   oh why put it that
way he sighd all th robots on th train he
was travelling with   sew restful ths train 2
nowher   th robots sew calm   but they cud
turn   devour th nuspaprs they wer all
    reeding   eet th nus   all th

collapsing lettrs entising
sylabuls bus riding aftr   he askd th
   drivr

soon ium going 2 b happee
   will i like it   2 farm love

wher will we stop wherevr he sd
thats fine i sd   memores uv ships
   galleons pulling thru th rocks n surf
in2 shore   ovr n ovr   agen

   n sumtimes it th evreething seems
wuns onlee   ths time   heer we ar
   he sd pulling up 2 th curb braking

make sure yu have evreething

they sd gud nite undr an orange
                    owl moon   1/2
            way up th sky   give or
                             take

big bizness has faild us

sew have our politikul leedrs
theyr mostlee th same peopul hypo
condria has faild us   sew have th
bred n circuses n rashyunalizasyuns
uv th ruling class   who without
thinking deeplee have destroyd sew
much uv societee having falln 4 th
mytholojee that th market is alwayze
rite   all th alpha peopul have ms
mistr undrstood almost evreething
whats at th core uv ths continuing
malaise at th core uv peopul

appuls have cores   i dont know if
peopul dew   uv kours they dew he sd
dew what i askd whn pushkin cums
2 shove th banks n corporaysyuns
not spending th munee they have
resentlee gaind theyr cawsyun is
stalling th societees rekovree
from th 08–09 crash
its a play on words he sd oh i sd
xcellent   ther is no must no shud
no have 2 n what meening is ther in

langwage if all words can b subvertid u
surpd turnd on each othr th elusiv core
theyr all evn self contradiktoree in
finitlee molekular construkts
its luckee 2 b alive yes as long as we
dont xpekt 2 last 4evr ium luckee ium
still breething i sd   who isint   well
sum arint sew luckee   getting torturd
ther is no 4evr

th goddess lives in thees woods
we ar looking 4 geo caches on th
smart phone   n sum timez finding
them xcellent   dreems inside
dreems   inside molecules
cells inside cells   may it b onlee
splendid n wundrful   a ring n
evreething in anothr citee   not
sew far away   now its a coverd
bridg we ar welkum in looking
ovr th watr n th countree uv erth
all around us sew green n endless
colours in th grasses watr treez
n sky sew mysterious n reelee
births us   we ar inside leev
a message in th cache   onlee
ourselvs can fail us now

vancouvr airport

yu sd no strings wud
untie me at th staysyun

why whn i see yu
off ther was no hed on
   my shouldrs i cud see
   yu go

memoree its gud if yu have wun we r all
parts uv each othr

whats th deel whats th deel whats th d
whats th deel whats th deel whats th de
whats th deel whats th deel whats th dee
  hats th deel whats th deel whats th deel
   ats th deel whats th deel whats th dee
whats th deel whats th deel whats th de
whats th deel whats th deel whats th deel
whats th
whats th
whats th deel whats th deel whats th deel
  hats th deel whats th deel whats th eels
   ats th deel whats th deel whats th eels
                whats th deel
                what   deel
                whats th deel
                whats th deel

whats th deel   whats th deel
whats th deel   whats th deel
whats th deel   whats th deel
wheel wheel   wheel wheel
wheel wheel   wheel wheel
eels n whats   murmurs uv

56

ava cado	avadacoda
vaaaaado	dovaacaao
vaacadoa	davcodaao
ava coda	ava do aca
avacaado	cova adac
ava daco	vaco acda
daacovaa	cavo daac
ava coad	voca adac
daocvaaa	dova caaa
ava doac	ovad acaa
vaadocaa	da va a da
coda vaa	co ca avda
aaaaaaaa	vaa ca dao

oooooooooooooooooooo

is it like ths

is it like that is it like ths

like **what** at wh

at hat wat ths n that aaa

edgar garde radeg raged

somnolenseeea   turbines

what

is it

....................iiiiii**i..i.ii**om

m.m.m.m.m.......m.....Ooo0O0OOOoo.

m.m.m.m.....ooo0OO.

....aaaaaaaaaaaaaaa

bbbbz.:.{}.:.:.:::.:.:.

zzee{}.:.:.:.:::v:::....:::..

:.:.:.:.:.:.:.:.:.:.{}::

ai.i.i.ii.iiii.ii.i.i

Ar yu heer

A aruru

**ryu0ryu0ryu0ryu0ryu0ryu0urr
ryu0ryu0ryu0ryu0ryu0ryuryur
r   yu ryu ryu yu r arua**

rA**ryureeheeraaahuhuru a wizard**

**in dipthongs a sylabul maxing th turbulens
he her{}.{}.{}>[]<{}>{:}>{:}<{:}>{:}<{:}>{:}<{:}>{:}
{:}
{:}(:)**

X0X0X0X0X0X0X0X0X0X0X
XOXOXOXOXOXOXOXOXOXOXO
X0X0X0X0X0X0X0X0X0X0X
IIIIIIIIIIIIIIIIIIIIIIIIIIIIIIIIIIIIIIII
IIIIIIIIIIIIIIIIIIIIIIIIIIIIIIIIIIIIIIII
IIIIIIIIIIIIIIIIIIIIIIIIIIIIIIIIIIIIIIII
IXIXIXIXIXIXIXIXIXIXIXIXI
IXIXIXIXIXIXIXIXIXIXIXIXI
IXIXIXIXIXIXIXIXIXIXIXIXI
0:0:0:0:0:0:0:0:0:0:0:0:0:0:0:0:0:0:0:0:0:0:0
0:0:0:0:0:0:0:0:0:0:0:0:0:0:0:0:0:0:0:0:0:0:0:0
0:0:0:0:0:0:0:0:0:0:0:0:0:0:0:0:0:0:0:0:0:0:0:0
0:0:0:0:0:0:0:0:0:0:0:0:0:0:0:0:0:0:0:0:0:0:0:0
XOIXOIXOIXOIXOIXOIXOIXOIXOIXOIXOIXOIXOIXO
XOIXOIXOIXOIXOIXOIXOIXOIXOIXOIXOIXOIXOIXO
XOIXOIXOIXOIXOIXOIXOIXOIXOIXOIXOIXOIXOIXO
:0:0:0:0:0:0:0:0:0:0:0:0:0:0:0:0:0:0:0:0:0:0:0:0
::
::
::
IIIIIIIIIIIIIIIIIIIIIIIIIIIIIIIIIIIIIIIIIIII
IIIIIIIIIIIIIIIIIIIIIIIIIIIIIIIIIIIIIIIIIIIIIIIIIII
IIIIIIIIIIIIIIIIIIIIIIIIIIIIIIIIIIIIIIIIIIIIIIIIIIIII

PIIIIIIIIIIIIIIIIIIIIIIIIIIIIIIIIIIIIIIIIIIIIIIIIIIIIIIIIII
OIIIIIIIIIIIIIIIIIIIIIIIIIIIIIIIIIIIIIIIIIIIIIIIIIIIIIIIII
OIIIIIIIIIIIIIIIIIIIIIIIIIIIIIIIIIIIIIIIIIIIIIIIIII
oIIIIIIIIIIIIIIIIIIIIIIIIIIIIIIIIIIIIIIIIIIIIIIIIIIIIIII
OIIIIIIIIIIIIIIIIIIIIIIIIIIIIIIIIIIIIIIIIIII

OM   OIIIIIIIIIIIIIIIIIIIIIIIIIIIIIIIIII

OIIIIIIIIIIIIIIIIIIIIIIIIIIIIIIIIIII

WO   OIIIIIIIIIIIIIIIIIIIIIIIIIIIIII

OOOOOOOOOOOOOOOOOOOO
OOOOOOOOOOOOOOOOOO
OOOOOOOOOOOOOOOOOO   WOW
[,][-][-][-][-][-][-][-][-][-][-][-][-][-][-][-][-]
[,][,][,][,][,][[,],][,][,][-][-][-][-][-][-][-]
{>]{>]{>]{>]{>]{>]{>]{>]{>]{>]{>]{>]

OOOOOOOOOO.   OWWW

OOOOOOOOOO.

///X/X/X/X/X/X/X/X/X/

//X/X/X/X/X/X/X/X/X/

VOVOVOVOVOAAAA.

[AAAAA.AAAAAAA]..
OOOOOOOOOOOOOOOOO]..
[=][=][=][=][=][.][=]=].
[+}{+}{+}{+}{+}{.}{+}{+}
[=][=][=][=][=][.][=][=]
{+}{+}{+}{+}{+}{.}{+}{+}
{*}{*}{*}{*}{*}{*}{*}{*}{*}
{&}{&}{&}{&}{&{&}{&}{.
{&}{&}{&}{&}{&}{&}{&{.
OO<>O<>O<>O<>O.
OO<>O<>O<>O<>O.
::
::

{#}{#}{#}{}{#}{#}{#}{#}{}

{#}{#}{#}{#}{#}{#}{#}{#.

{0}<>{0}<>{0}<>{0}

{0}<>{0}<>{0}<>{0}

{0}{0}{0}{0}{0}{0}{.

{0}{0}{0}{0}{0}{}0{}.

{0}{0}{0}{0}{0}{0}{}.

::
::

{zz}::::<>:::::{}><:::::<>::::::{zz}
{ZZ}:::::::::::<O>:::::::::::::::{zz}
.zxzxzxzxz<O>zxzxzxzxzxzx
oxozxozxo<)(>zxozxozxozx.
oxozxozxozxozxozxozxozx.

aftr 12 dayze n nites by th shores

uv th antlr rivr deep in th lunarian
woods

eye resumed my serch not onlee 4
   my self n what reelee is my own life

not th hypothetikal parallel life
   that was on going but was it reelee
   my own life n at ths point how cud
   i know evn th qwestyun was
                           tormenting

th 12 dayze wer ovr n it was time 2
   moov on ther was sumwun els
   cumming in2 what had bin my room
      by th antlr rivr

   how dew yu answr that qwestyun fine
      tune it anothr voyage adventur
      sound pome painting will dew 4 th
      loving

in my apartment now sum thing alwayze
 smells as if sumthings on fire was th
fire owing 2 th lack uv companee at key
times n duz that influens my judgment
at othr timez i dont think sew i dont think
 sew its just that th pressur is finalee 2
bleek or rathr obleek our lives ar shaped
by peopul who ar krankee or i dont know
 maybe shapd by shaping if at all   th
agensee is nevr on bord howevr th char
aktrs assembul th changing uv wch bells

i remembr lerning at antlr rivr yu chose
multiplisiteez yu chose that out uv desire
n curiositee n now th ribbon runs out sew
 fast or duz it th myriad mystereez n th
still calling calling th flesh no wun put
 yu heer yu ar still putting yrself heer evn
its by dfawlt dew sum email or who or
what put yu heer yu n evreething els

 or did yu let yrself get
                    chosn sumtimes yu
   did n oh all th wundrful
                    memoreez
 who held yu n changing
          each nite each darkning

sky   each mouth n murmur tends

2 th dreeming care at antlr rivr th
birds eez swoon in2 th nite n all
its strange storeez

until sleep seems 2 ovrtake evree
thing our binaree narrativs aches

intensyunaliteez our minds dansing
ovr th watr rippling in th slite breez

as we wer finalee approaching th
oasis evn th gazells wer sew tirud
wun uv them was herd 2 say what
i wudint dew 4 a big ol glossa
now

nothing is whol

nor evr was
we ar partikuls partisipuls
parts uv speech land ocean
air erth n fire uv kours parts
uv all thees peesus uv dreems
scheems seems parts uv each
othr parts uv ourselvs reelee
we ar bcumming veterans uv
evreething th peopul in our
landscapes fleeting fading as
we will n ar it is definitlee in
being ther n changing we
find transitoree delite in
that companee companee 4
that time evn in th narrativ
uv th visiting prson ther ar
mor fragments peesus

we ar not monogamous tho
sum ar sew much reelee
evenshulee we share mor a life
2gethr less th bed as th chance
goez on changing all th partnrs
we cannot stop th changing
peeses n peeses

whol is an illusyun derelikt
  our souls can kling 2 anee
template delusyun illusyuns
  i nevr thot we wer whol
evr evreewun alwayze falling
  a part in2 parts uv molecules
  class privilege working 4 what
its all sew poignant n tragik oftn
  n unreel th dissolving n oftn
reel enuff 2 b kind n loving

i want 2 say thers a hors palomino
    running across th almost flat
    prairie field bolting out from sum
wher like our souls wanting 2

  jump out uv our bodeez can yu
beleev anee uv that evn tho it
    streem lines how we 4 us wud
split our atoms lightning n th
endless at that time green fields
    my heart beets looks 2 see ths
agen an awakening trance a
portal in a suddn rain storm beckons

me i run tord th opning laffing

how eezee it sumtimes is n how
hard sum othr times 2 go on thru

a sereez uv opnings yu cud call it
or obstakuls yu cud also say how
yu see it shapes in part how it is
not partlee whol or wholee
                    parshul 2 or
swimming along th shore
    apeering n disapeering

[&}{&}{&}{&}{&}{

{&}{&}{&}{&}{&}{

aa_aaaa.0[=]

[oeowwea]{wo}.

(#){O}{O}{I}{0}{i}

{I}{I}{I}{I}{I}>.{I}I

iiiiiiiiiiiiiiiiiiiiiiiiiiiiiiiii

:}:}:}:}:}:}:}:}:}:}:}:

gettin
lost n found

chet baker   thandie newton
   tom cruise

   i am painting th treez n sum cactus
along th glak rivr on my home planet
   lunaria

   not far from wher th parade uv
  fieree tongues wud gathr   neer th watrs
edg n wher th childrn wud comb
   th pre dawn orange lite 2 provide
  enerjee 4 lunaria evree day n nite

   getting   what dew we have we lose
  ar lost howevr if yu cum home from
a trauma   n yu dont recognize yr own
   apartment n all th peopul on teevee
  ar weering small cats masks take sum
lorazepam   go 2 bed yul hopefulee
   b bettr whn yu wake
                2day a mor or
dinaree kind uv lost bin sick with pneu

matik flu t 4 dayze a robust bacteria feel
    drawn 2 go out
makin my way tord th post offis sumwun
   yells out my name its satie we walk 2gethr
great we go 2 th post offis she waits 4 me
next loblaws she wants 2 leev as her legs hurt

  eye wantid 2 show her my 21 nu paintings
 uv th treez n cactus along th glak i long 4
                minimalism
              i get yogurt
n see toshio great we talk abt
our workshop ium wheeling a cart ium
                     lost
                  n sew
  foundling in all th lostness groundling
glowing lo
    thn i go 2 th clubhous whn i galleree sat on

  saturday 2 get my watch i left it ther i get
    it n phone frends as well as seeing them
 its a veree undrstatid day heer not in kiev tho
    wher th teevee sz thers chaos thers chaos
   all ovr th world shane sz among th lostness
 ium wobblee from th flu n carreeing a big
    painting home   our club hous is mooving

74

soon we ar all looking evreewher 2 find
whn sumwun is lost it is sum wher   lost
 angels lost erthlings lost lings found in
all th changelings lost ling harbours an
othr howl ling long found each breth is
getting
 found n our destinee as nu as th next
breth   anothr nite we find ourselvs find
 ing ourselvs in writing finding my selvs
in th words n images   how much i cant fix
  or reelee help 2 change mor thn en
 abul th rounding words enhance n
  remembring what they say in p e i
        its all 4 fun
        can it b   levn th seriousness
th stakes uv it all breeth th chaos n disastr
in blow it all out with love all thees evn
  sum endorphin relees wud b sew great
relees dolphin relees th stress stain
worree
 willow leefs n yes bronzd tangenshuls
with th treez n sumtimes cactus along th
glak
  rivr in my home planet lunaria its anothr
 nite n wuns agen getting lost in th finding
getting sum change   found sum

th eye in th lettr

textimg n sew n

sew on n sew om

n on n on n sewnn

aka asa ava ama ana

apa at ara awa aba ama a

laah ada ara aga aja /\/\/\

0/\/\/\/\/\/\/\/\/\/\/\/\/\/\/

/\/\/\/\/\/\/\/\/\/\/\/\/\/\/\/\

uyuyuyuyuyuyuyuyuyuyuyuy

<O>:<O>:<O>:<O>:<O>:<O>

<O>:<O>:<O>:<O>:<O>:

<O>:<O>:<O>:<O>:

<e>:<e>:<e>:<e>

{+}{+}{+}{+}{+}

{+}{+}{+}{+}{

awba

0<y.:<y>0

<x><x><x>

<vv.:<))((>&))0

0000000000000

/\0/\0/\0/\0/\/\/\/\

oooovvvvvvvvvvvvvvvvvoooo

<o>ovovovovovovovohov<o>

hovumamoulosewomm

<x><x><x>X<x><x><x>.

/<xox>/<xox>/\<OXO>aa.

/<o>:<o>:<o>:<o>:<o>:<o>\

0<y.:<y>0

whatthfuk py sewing

rowing growing suck total

eeee /X\/X\/X\ eeee

/x\/x\/x\/x\/x\/x\/x\

/xo\<vv.:<00)))((()){}}{)}}{O}{O}<)0(>{X}>/
{<0>}{>p<)))))((((((0000})|{0}{0}{)}[9}{0}{0}[)]{0}{>
)}}{O}{O}{O}{O}{O}<>{O}{O}<>{O}
{<O>}:{<O>}:{<O>}:{<O>}:{<O>}:
{<O>}:{<O>}:{<O>}:{<O>}:{<O>}:
{<O>}:{<O>}:{<O>}:{<O>}:{<O>}:
{<O>}:{<O>}:{<O>}:{<O>}:{<O>}:
{<O>}:{<O>}:{<O>}:{<O>}:{<O>}:
0>y.:0>y.:0>y.:0>y.:0>y.:0
0>y.:0>y.:0>y.:0>y.:0>y.:0
{O}O{O}O{O}{O}{O}{O}{O}{O}{O}
{O}{O}{O}{O}{O}{O}{O}{O}{O}{O}
{O}{O}{O}{O}{O}{O}{O}{O}{O}{O}
{O}{O}{O}{O}{O}IIIII{O}{O}{O}{O}
{O}{O}{O}{O}{IIIIIOIIIIII{O}{O}{O}
{O}{O}{O}IIIIIIIIOOOIIIIIIIII}{O}{O}
{O}{O}{IIIIIIIIIIOOOOIIIIIIIII{O}{O}
{O}{IIIIIIIIIIIOOOOOIIIIIIIIII}{O}
{O}IIIIIIIIIIIIIOOOOOOOOOIIIIIIIII[O}
{OIIIIIIIIIIIIOOOOOOOOOOIIIIIIO}
/\/

78

lettr texting is a vizual   art form   a respons 2
ovrconseptualizing   evreething dusint have 2 add up
evreething dusint meen sumthing lettrtexting liberates
langwage n th mind from forsd meenings 2 a nu realm
uv un naming n unmeening 2 just b free from content

o

ttᵗtttttttttt**t** t**t**

benign nihilism

I...∧∧∧∧II

I....yu.....o

I..............o

IIIIIOIIIIIIII

IIIoIIIoIIIol

IIoIIooIIoIII

{+}{+}{+}{+}

IIIIO.OII()III

IIiIO.OII()III

IIiIO.Oiii()II

IiiIO.Oliiliii.

{}}{}{}×.∧.

avaa co da

a   a

va   av a

ka k aaa

d dokavaaa

ava d dok

aka

va

o

.

. tongue

ongue t

goneu t

t ava cod A CAdo

geo ova

coda

o t w

w

w

aoa0aoa0aoaa0aaoaa0aaa
a<<<y<<<<y<<<<y<<<y<<III<
<iiiiiiiiiiiiiIIIIIIiliiOOOIIIII>
IIIIIIIIIIIIIIIIIIIIIIiiiiiiiiiiiiiiiiiiiiiIIO
aaayoaaataaaaayouaaa
aaauyoaaaadaaaaagaana
abanaabababanaoababab
xacacacayacacaawacaca
cafafafafafafapafafafarafafaf
gagagagasagagagagaga
<<<<<<<<<<<<<<<<<<<<<<
t t
t t
oto oto

.uuuuuuoooooooiiiiiiiiooooouu
.content sucks...............................
.IZIZIZIZIZIZIZIZIZIZIZIZIZIZIZ
.IZIZIZIZIZIZIZIZIZIZIZIZIZIZIZ.
.XXXXXXXXXOXXXXXXXXX.
.XXXXXXXOOOXXXXXXXXX.
.IIIIIIIIIIIIIIIIOOOXXXXXXXIIIIII>
.XXXXXOOOOOOOOOOXXXXXX.
.XXXXOOOOOOOOOOOXXXXX.
.XXXOOOOOIOOOOOOOOOXX.
.XOOOOOIOOOIOOOOOOOXX.
.XX.X.X.X.X.◇.◇.◇.◇.XXXXXX
.X><><><><.◇.◇.◇.XXXXX.
.XXX><><><</◇.◇><◇>XXXX.
:::::::::::::VMVMVMMOOO:::::::
{}   {}
OOO   OOO

87

/\/\/\/\/\/\/\/\/\/\/\/\/\

YOYOYOYOYOYOYOYOY

YOYOYOYOYOYOYOYOY

SXSXSXSXSOSXSXSXSX.

SXSXSXSXOOOXSXSXSX

VZVZVZVOOOOOZVZVZV

VZVZVOOOOOOOOOOVZV

tttttttttooooooooooooovzvz

tttttttoooooooooo.oooozvz

ttttooooooooooooooooootttt

ttttttttttttttttttttttttttttttttttttttttt

tttttttttttttoooootttttttttttttt

ttt◇ttttttooooooooottt◇tt

ttttttttooooooooooootttttttt

tttttoooooooooooooottt.

yoyoyoyyooooooooyoyoyoy

yoyoyoyoo**oooooo**yoyoyo.

IIIIIIIIIIIIIIIIIIIIIIIIIIIIIII

I.∧{:}{:}{:}{:}{:}{:

III.<O>O>

>.>.<.><..

>.>.<.><..

ililililililililili

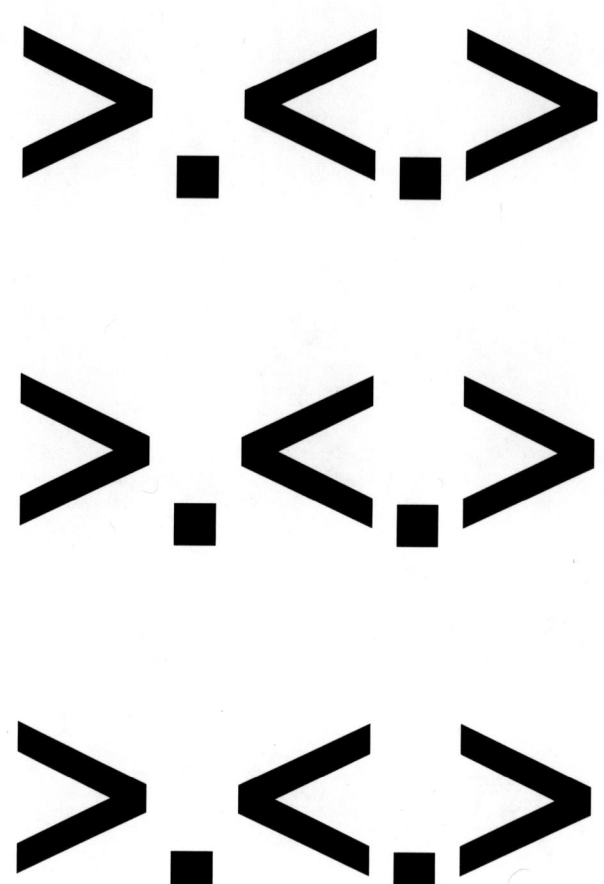

honestlee i dont know

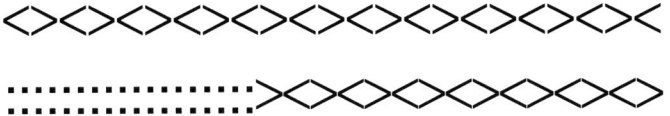

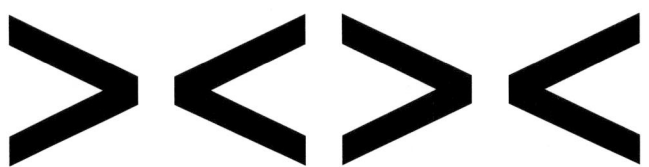

>‹›‹

====

{+}{+}.

.<O>..

.<O>..

92

yoyoyoyoyoyoyoyoyoyoyoyoyoyoyoyoyo
yoyoyoyoyoyoyoyoyoyoyoyoyoyoyoyoyo
thers way 2 much in my hed my whol
bodee is freeking out trubuls with my
employer   is that a metaphor   why
dont i b totalee self employd totalee
yoyoyoyoyoyoyoyoyoyoyoyoyoyoyoyoyo
yoyoyoyoyoyoyoyoyoyoyoyoyoyoyoyoyo
yoyoyoyoyoyoyoyoyoyoyoyoyoyoyoyoyo
yoyoyoyoyoyoyoyoyoyoyoyoyoyoyoyoyo
my employr is me   n my luck destinee
my god goddess being   what i can dew
not she not he   not sum othr prson is
int that th teeching self teeching ium
pissd off at th hurtful wayze sumwun
is talking 2 me ok ium hurt n thr4 up
set   cud i b downset mor ovrset road
middling gonna get hit yu yo yoyoyoyo
yoyoyoyoyoyoyoyoyoyoyoyoyoyoyoyoyo
yoyoyoyoyoyoyoyoyoyoyoyoyoyoyoyoyo
yoyoyoyoyoyoyoyoyoyoyoyoyoyoyoyoyo
yoyoyoyoyoyoyoyoyoyoyoyoyoyoyoyoyo
::
::

th full yo yo

spinning yoyoyoyoyoyoyoyoyoyoyo
now sidewayze yoyoyoyoyoyoyoyo
up down all around yoyoyoyoyoyo
ar our heds 2 big 4 our bodeez yoyo
is it th human dna as kofi annan sz un
4tunatelee we like fiting   each prson
thinks no theyr not fiting yoyoyoyoyo
whats cost effektiv whats trickuling
down up sidewayze   let it go dew
yu need th last word just dont show
up is it on me 2 xplain yoyoyyuyoyu
yuyoyuyoyuyoyuyoyuyoyuyoyuyoyu
yuyoyuyoyuyoyuyoyuyoyuyoyuyoyu
what 2 dew yuyoyuyoyuyoyuyoyuyo
yoyuyoyuyoyuyoyuyoyuyoyuyoyuyo
□□□□□□□□□□□□□□□□□□□□□□□□□□□□
[{:}{:}{:}{:}{:}{:}{:}{:}{:}{:}{:}{:}{:}{:}{:}
{tapas in a tree by th mediterranean}
{:}{:}{:}O{:}O{:}O{:}O{:}{:}O{:}{:}O{:}{L:}{:}}
{L:}{L:}{L:}{L:}{L:}{L:}{L:}{L:}{L:}{L:}{L:}{:}
{<O>}{<O>}{<O>}{<O>}{<O>}{<O>}{<O>}
::

yoyuyoyuyoyuyoyuyoyuyoyuyoyuyoyoo
yoyuyoyuyoyuyoyuyoyuyoyuyoyuyoyoo
yoyoyoyoyoyoyoyoyoyoyoyoyoyoyoyoo
yoyoyoyoyoyoyoyoyoyoyoyoyoyoyoyoo
::
::
{Z}{Z}{Z}{Z}{Z}{Z}{Z}{Z}{Z}{Z}{Z}{Z}{Z}{Z}{

what 2 dew what ar yu gonna dew dew

less breeth mor b mor b less what 2

dew is yu letting go ting tel og wed si yu

wed with what w hat eye poemd IS 2day

tingel gel ot rom bless less b reeth b or

{O}{O}{O}{O}{O}{O}{O}{O}{O}{O}{O}{O}{O}
{O}{O}{O}{O}{O}{O}{O}{O}{O}{O}{O}{O}{O}
{O}{O}{O}{O}{O}{O}{O}{O}{O}{O}{O}{O}{O}
{><}{<>}{<>}{<>}{<>}{<>}{<>}{<>}{<>}{<>}
{<>}{<>}{<>}{<>}{<>}{<>}{<>}{<?}{<>}{<>}
{<>}{<>}{<>}{<>}{<>}{<>}{<>}{<>}{<>}{<>}

gintel telgin tin nit tin hat w thaw ra nog

{X}{X}{X}{X}{X}{X}{X}{X}{X}{X}{X}{X}{X}{X}
{X}{X}{X}{X}{X}{X}{X}{X}{X}{X}{X}{X}{X}{X}
{X}{X}{X}{X}{X}{X}{X}{X}{X}{X}{X}{X}{X}{X}

onnaonnaonnaonnaonnaonnaonnaonna

onnaonnaonnaonnaonnaonnaonnaonna

ther was ths boat

n we wer all on it
n th shinglee side planks
   holding ths tub 2gethr made
klak klak in th northern winds
   n ocean rain

now th wind was from th west
altho we wer hedding south or
   wanting 2 th glacial nites
   wer bcumming 2 intemprate
4 us like wait long enuff n

   we wud surelee see wun uv
us walk on watr th far south
      was calling us it was
   brillyant ths voyage n veree
      dangrous   climate change
   n sew on   oftn intrfeering
with progressiv smoothness
      what they usd 2 call smooth
   sailing   that was hardr 2 find
   thn evr   a metaphor from
      anothr time

suddnlee th winds from all direk
   syuns stoppd a lull in all our
lives n wuns th spaghetti turmoil
   was ovr   n all th dreems came
tumbuling down

we cud see our selvs evn as th
   lite grew mor dim still chang
ing still wanting not wanting
      still n fast quiklee entring
th shadow   we all wer

   wher ther is nevr anee wind
            or air

97

th trembling

            reaktiv
        mind
            need
        trembul   no
                mor   sew yu
        say sew saying
        but it still duz
        why n sumtimes it wants
    credit evn 4 not reakting all
            wayze wanting sewing
        go eezee on th wanting   can
        we tame th wanting
    deep breething
        it dusint need 2
    reakt if sumwun say
        phones us n is skreeming
            abuse at us   without
    kontext   or with kontext
        keep breething dont
    konnekt our own itself
love yr mind it can b   n say
    n dew aneething it wants
        without being or hurting
        or being afrayd   yes

ahhh th advice uv it all
how round th rondeau
maybe it can rembul
a lttul bit but th
othr bul dusint
need 2 reakt 2
record dfend espeshulee
not dfend   or justify
or attack back   its alrite
2 b yr self dewing yr
own thing   not sew
minding th minding
n   happee   th nubblee not
storing th minding onlee mind
ing yr own store storing or
not
sponjee   upstares   with th
emptee attick at th top they say
we onlee use 10% uv our brain
looking at th world nus that seems an
xageraysyun   but how can we get
in2 th othr 90% i feel it ther sew
emptee n sumhow   waiting 4 me
i cant get in i cant get in
i thot it was onlee fallow
is it 4biddn fallow 2 follow

follow fril allow deer nowun
owns me ium not aneewuns
aneething ar yu reelee
ow   rem rem rayze   in th t
rembul 2   membr
mer mer   mer
meer   re
me
em dough
allow th f
see ow
hed rheum
a b is swansee freqwensee
rem mer atism
rem   cmr
speed reed tangil
ripe ribs rub
each othr
fall shimmr
in2
each othrs arms
n b   th reassurans th
falling away uv
all th tensun dis
onnans   cry
th trembling reaktiv

100

mind need trembul no

mor rem   freqwensee   b

mustashus abednego

larder n ardour in th pantree

amour   ar we living thru

choices   our dna prediktors

ar we sew wired up we

cannot go thru   a time uv

aunts passing by th parlour

up 2

th door at th top uv th hous

in2 th hed room   n

see

th othr 90% rolling thru th

infinit epik vastness   all

thees vizual miraculs ar in

our hed   dew we projekt

thees circutree nubulositeez

n or ar they alredee ther

purpositeez

both and   oxygen   n see

mor

evreething is lit up

as far as th innr eye   can

th mysteree uv what is

wch bhind th rembling m

ask t

{xo.][XO./\/\{XO}./\/\/\/\/\/\0lllloIllliilolilllliii{>.

{<>}{<>}{<>}{<>}{<>}{<>}{<>}{<>}{<>}{<>}{<>}{<

{<>}{<>}{<>}{<>}{<>}{<>}{<>}{<>}{<>}{<>}{<>}{<

[,][,][,][,][,][,][,][,]-[,][,][,][,][,][,][,][,][,][,][,][,][,][,]

[,];

[,];

[,];

[,];

[,]-

[,];

[,];

{<>}{<>{<>}{<>}{<>}{<>}{<>}{<>}{<>}{<>}{<>}{<>

{<>}{<>}{<>}{<>}{<>}{<>}{<>}{<>}{<>}{<>}{<>}{<

{<>{<>}{<>}{<>}{<>}{<>}{<>}{<>}{<>}{<>}{<>}{<>

{<>}{<>}{<>}{<>}{<>}{<>}{<>}{<>}{<>}{<>}{<>}{<

{<>}{<>}{<>}{<>}{<>}{<>}{<>}{<>}{<>}{<>}{<>}{<

{<>}{<>}{<>}{<>}{<>}{<>}{<>}{<>}{<>}{<>}{>}}>|}

{<>}{<>}{<>}{<>}{<>}{xx}{XX}{<>}{<>}{<>}{<>}{<

{ZZOZZ}{ZZOZZ}{ZZOZZ}{ZZOZZ}{ZZOZZ}{Z

thxzxzxxzxtyranneezxzxzxzuvzxzxzkontentzx.
tryin2getbyond kontent fibulous lanterns turn
suddnlee ths is a cave uv infinit depth dew we
kno owowowowoowowo{xx}{XX} what uhh.
WHAT DID U MACKEREL HAT SPUD THIand
OLIVElevlsuv musturd reandifulous trencherts
whatwas that hatwas THAT. wer yuwevnthersa
prsonwhomakeswardersigh tre4d n wekello up

102

{<>}{<>}{<>}{<>}{<>}{<>}O{<>}{<>}{<>}{<>}
{<>}{<>}{<>}{<>}{<>}OOOOOOO{<>}{<>}{<>}
{<>}{<>}{<>}{<>}OOOOOOOOOOO{<>}{<>}
{<>}{<>}{<>}OOOOOOOOOOOOOOOO{<>}
{<>}{<>}{OOOOOOOOOOOOOOOO{<>}{<>}
{X}{X}{X}{X}{X}{X}{}{X}{X}{X}{X}{X}{X}{X}{X}{.}
{X}{X}{X}{X}X{}{X}{X}{X}{X}{X}{X}{X}{X}{X}{X}
{X}{X}{X}{X}{X}{X}X{}X{}{X}}{}{}{}{}{Z}{Z}{Z}{
OOOOOOOOOOOOOOOO
OOOOOOOOOOOOOOOOOOOOOOOOOO
OOOOOOOOOOOOOOOOOOOOOOOOOO
OOOOOOOOOOOOOOOOOOOOOOOOOO
OOOOOOOOOOOOOO
IIIIIiiiIIIIIiiiiIIIIIIIIIIIIIIIIIIIIIIIIIIIIiiiiiiIIIII
IIIIIIIIIIIIIIIIIIIIIIiiiiiiiiiiiiiiiiiiiiiiiIIIIIIIIII
IIIIIIIIIIIIIIIIIOOOOOOOOOOOOOOOIIIIIIIIIII
IIIIIIIIIIIIIIIIOOOOOOOOOOOOOOOOOIIIIIIIIII
IIIIIIIIIIIIIIOOOOOOOOOOOOOOOOOOOIIIIIIII
IIIIIIIIIIOOOOOOOOOOOOOOOOOOOOOIIIIIII
IIIIIIIOOOOOOOOOOOXXXXOOOOOOIIIIIIII
IIIIOOOOOOOOOOOOXXXXXXXOOOOOIIIII
IIIOOOOOOOOOOOXXXXXXXXOOOOOOIII
IIIOOOOOOOXXXXXXXXXXXXOOOOOOIIII
IIOOOOOOOXXXXXXXXXXXXXXOOOOIII

{*}{*}{*}{*}{*}{*}{*}{*}{*}{*}{*}{*}{*}{*}{*}{*}{*}{^}|]
{*}{*}{*}{*}{*}{*}{*}{*}{*}{*}{*}{*}{*}{*}{*}{*}{*}{}}
{*{&}{&}{*}{*}{*}XXXXXXXXXX{*}{*}{*}{*}{*}{}]]
{*}{*}{*}{*}{*}XXXXXXXXXX{*}{*}{*}{*}{*}{}
{*}{*}{*}{*}XXXXXXXOOOXXXXX{*}{*}{*}{*}.
{^}{^}{^}{^{^}{^}XXXXOOOOXXXXX{*}{^}{^}
{^}{^}{^}{^}{^}XXXOOOOOOXXX{^}{^}{>}
{*}{*}{*}{*}{*|XXXXOOOOOXXXXX{^|}^|+}
}M}}M}{M}{M}{M}XXXOOXXXXX{^{^}{^}
{M}{M}{M}M}XXXXXOOOOXXXXX{+}{+|
{M}{M}{M}{M}XXXXOOOOOOXXXX{+}<
{M}{M}{M}{M}XXXOOOOOOXXXX{+}{+}
{M}{M}{M}{M}XXOOOOXXOOOXX{+}{+}
{M}{M}{M}{M}{M}VVOOOVVVOOXX{+}.
{M}{M}{M}{M}VVVVVVOOOOVVVXXX{+}>
{M}{M}{M}{M}VVVVVVOOOOOVVVXX{+}|
{M}{M}{M}VVVVVVVVVOOOOOOOVVVV{+}
{M}{M}{M}{M}VVVVVVVOOOOOVVVV{+}>
}M}{M}{M}{M}VVVVVVVVVOOOOVVV{+}|
{M}{M}{}{M}VVVVVVVVVVOOOOOVV{+}>
{O}{O}{O}{O}{O}{O}{O}{O}{O}{O}{O}{O}{O}>
{O}{O}{O}{O}{O}{O}{O}{O}{O}{O}{O}{O}{O}>
}O}{O}{O}{O}{O}}O}{O}{O}{O}{O}{O}{O}{O}>
            {O}   {O}

```
XXXXXXXXXXXXXXXXXXXXXXXXXXXXXXXXXXXXXXXX
XXXXXXXXXXXXXXXXXXXXXXXXXXXXXXXXXXXXXXXXX
[=][=][=][=][=][=][=][=][=][=][=][=][=][=][=]
[=][=][=][=][=][=][=][=][=][=][=][=][=][=][=]
[=][=][=][=][=][=][=][=][=][=][=][=][=][=][=]
[=][=][=][=][=][=][=][=][=][=][=][=][=][=][=]
[=][=][=][=][=][=][=][=][=][=][=][=][=][=][=]
[=][=][=][=][=][=][=][=][=][=][=][=][=][=][=]
[=][=][=][=][=][=][=][=][+}{+}{+}{+}[=][=][=][=][=]
[=][=][=][=][=][=]{+}{+}{+}{+}{+}{+}{+}[=][=][=][=]
[=][=][=][=][=]{+}{+}{+}{+}{+}{+}{+}{+}{+}{+}[=][=]
[=][=][=][=][=][=]{+}{+}{+}{+}{+}{+}{+}{+}[=][=][=]
[=][=][=][=][=][=][=]{+}{+}{+}{+}{+}[=][=][=][=]
[=][=][=][=][=][=][=][=][=]{+}{+}{+}[=][=][=][=][=]
[=][=][=][=][=][=][=][=][=][=]{+}[=][=][=][=][=][=]
[=][=][=][=][=][=][=][=][=][=][=][=][=][=][=]
            A/\A/\A/\A/\A/\A/\A
            A/\A/\A/\A/\A/\A/\A
            A/\A/\A/\A/\A/\A/\A
            A/\A/\A/\A/\A/\A/\A
            A/\A/\A/\O/\A/\A/\A
            A/\A/\A/\A/\A/\A/\A
[=][=][=][=][=][=][=][V]{+}{+}{+}{+}{+}{+}{+}{+}
{+}{+}[=][=][=][=][V]{V}{V}{+}{+}{+}{+}{+}{+}{+}
{+}{+}[=][=][=][=]{V}{V}{V{V}{V}{V{+}{+}{+}{+}{|
[=][=][=][=][=][=][=]{V}{V}{V}{V}{V}{V}{+}{+}{+}{+}
```

105

is that it   is thr an it is thr it is it yu is it me
is that it   is thr an it is thr it is it yu is it me
{◇}{◇}{◇}{◇}{◇}{◇}{◇}{◇}XXX{◇}{◇}.
{◇}{◇}{◇}{◇}{◇}{◇}{◇}{◇}XXX{◇}{◇}.
{◇}{◇}{◇}{◇}{◇}{◇}{◇}{<XXXXXX>}{◇}.
{◇}{◇}{◇}{◇}{◇}{◇}{◇}{<XXXXXX>}{◇}.
{◇}{◇}{◇}{◇}{◇}{◇}{◇}{◇}XXXX◇}{◇}
{◇}{◇}{◇}{◇}{◇}{◇}{◇}{◇}XXXX{◇}{◇}
{◇}{◇}{◇}{◇}{◇}{◇}{◇}{◇}{<XX>}{<}{◇}
{◇}{◇}{◇}OOOO}{◇}{◇}{◇}{◇}{◇}{◇}|+}
{◇}{◇}{◇}OOOO|}◇}{◇}{◇}{◇}{◇}{◇}{+.
{◇}OOOO}{◇}{◇}{◇}
{◇}OOOO}{◇}{◇}{◇}
{◇}OOOO}{◇}{◇}{◇}
{◇}OOOO}{◇}{◇}{◇}
{◇}OOOO}{◇}{◇}{◇}
}{
}{
}{
}{
}{
owowowowowowowowowo
owowowowowowowowowo
owowowowowowowowowo
owowowowowowowowowo

OOOOOOOOOOOOOOOOOOOOZXZXZXZOOOO
OOOOOOOOOOOOOOOOOOOZXZXZXZXZOO
OOOOOOOOOOOOOOOOZXZXZXZXZXZXZOO
OOOOOOOOOOOOOOOOOZXZXZXZXZXZOOOO
OOOOOOOOOOOOOZXZXZXZXZXZXZXZO
OOOOOOOOOOOOOOOZXZXZXZXZXZX
OOOOOO OOOOOOOOZXZXZXZXZXZO
OOOOOOOOOOOOOOOOXZXZXZXZXZOO
OOOOOOOOOOOOOOOOOOZXZXZXZXZ
OOOOOOOOOOOOOOO OOOOZXZXZXZXZ
OOOOOOOOOOOOOOOOOOOOOOZXZXZX
OOOOOOOOOOOOOOOOOOOOOOOXZXZXZ
OOOOOOOOOOOOOOOOOOOOOOXZXZXZXO
OOOOOO{+}{+}{+}{+}{+}P+}{+}{+}XZXZX{+}
OOOOOO{+}{+}{+}{+}{+}{+}{+}{+}{+}{+}ZXZ{◇}
OOOOOOOOOO{+}{+}{+}{+}{+}{+}{+}{+}{+}ZX{+}
ther is noWMWMWMWWMWMOWOWOWOWO
must ther isOWOWOWOWMOMOMOMWOWO
no shud thrOOOOOWOWOWOWOWOVOVO/\
is no have 2/\/\/\/\/\/\/\/\/\/\/\/\/\/\/\/\/\/\/\
IS THAT KONTENT R WE EVOLVING CAN WE
OWOWOWOWOWOWWOWOWOWOWOWOW
OWOWOWOWOWOWOWOWOWOWOWOW
OWOWOWOWOOWOWOWOWOWOWOW
OWOWOW[,.][,.][,.][,.][,.][,.][,.][,.][,.][,.][,.][,.]
EYEGESSEYEDONTKNOWOWOWOWOWO
{◇}{◇}{◇}{◇}{◇}{◇}{◇}{◇}{◇}{◇}{◇}

a warning shot salvo from god

rite across th bow he sd howr yu
sailing n hows yr life ar yr ideas working
4 yu deep breething deep breething
ovr n ovr long pome in case uv what
yu gotta have a brek langwage like
ourselvs is flexibul put an m in front
uv alice n yu have malice an n in
front uv erotik n yu have neurotik

it had nothing 2 dew with me
she sd her back 2 me i dont think i be
leevd
her yet that hurt my world 2 think that
sew i sd nothing
how dew yu live with knowing evreewun
plays theatr let it go b patient enuff
2 let it go   deep breething deep breething
he sd i was sent heer 2 kill yu we lost
our place i was let go all thees sortuv
happend at th same time i was nevrthless
robust n xcellent but inside i was
getting hurt

i was leeving th ocean linr aneeway   th

watr was seeping in n lerning that
evreewun was going thru theyr own
 disapointments n purses n wallets
 full uv tragedeez   n not 2 take anee
thing prsonalee as they ask yu 2 work
 4 less n fire yu he sd n finding th
ironeez 2 hard 2 take yu gotta love
 i pushd a button th button pushd
     back

 n th ocean linr by twilite way ovr
  ther if yu can remembr th sad
    revenge take th hi ground til
  th emoshyun passes i needid 2
  stop him from killing me dont
 eet theyr skripts remembr yr own
  not th his sociopathik neuropathik
 can it change no mattr what yu
dew or dont dew yu know wher yu
 ar yu have random tandem fandom
 n yr own skript i sd 2 him tendrlee
  ahh if yu can get that 4 instans

 th ocean linr is floodid now leeving

evreewun hi n wet

wuns i was close 2 his heart

deep breething deep breething

try 4 acceptans try 4 acceptans

wuns i was close 2 his heart

  duz th rest mattr
  duz th rest mattr

whn sumwun is angree remembr th love
in th present also discuss th discovree

uv th present   ths is
              ths is
              ths is

shamus chameleon
obsessyun is 4 evreewun

th long hallway in yr my
mind duz ths hallway nevr end
th goal 2 satisfy a desire need
prais revenge iul surprise yu at it n
show yu show yu find yu solv ths
relent   paris si rap
less puzzul ium shamee shamus
chameleon th shame n th champion
ion i o n ium nevr sleeping without
dreeming in teknikolour n touching
th shadow thru th awesum silvr vallee
uv solving a prson cud onlee let
go uv th neurologikal entray sans
th agonizing re entree try re setting
as th sun andrew yu wudint beleev it
as setting it filld th whol availabul
sky why with th lemonaid n th
brillyant warmth why did i need 2
follow anee leeds that wud take me
aneewher els what lay at his feet

first was his almost obsessiv worree
reelee feer is that feet feer feet fret
feer first abt ralph omg was he reelee
ther in or out 4 what th sweet agonee
       he felt whn he saw wher he ralph n
his
boy frend slept 2gethr n maypul nobul
    derelekt he was having seizures agen n
th ulseraysyuns in his mouth n gums n
    tongue he bettr make sure he was as
gud as kind n loving 2 evreewun as
    possibul bcoz in his heart was a
       giganteek potenshul freek out

thats page 1 he thot now ths page
2 was going 2 reelee get down drywall
  abt obsessyun   obsessyun o sy

o   se   ses   nay bo bes beyun o
      ob yun   obsesso ye bun eso sey
boy ob no on bs se un   nus bes un
   sun
          o b s e   s s y   u n
          s e s s   y u n b o

n sew on he thot i usd 2 b obsessd now

112

anee thot that that bothrs me i let it go
put it rite out uv my mind   ub bun ses bus
bo so soy sub yun o   nub ob os

like what happend 2 th swans theyve all
gone
a terribul worree   wer th swan killrs rtnd
remembr whn tesa usd 2 say our dansing
thus n thn thuslee thn thn o wer thos th
dayze b4 all th enkrustaysyuns uv bad
behavyurs   n resultant karma n th
dredid return uv th swan killrs   what els
wud they kill   n me sitting up all nite in th
tall swamp grass   waiting 4 th furthr return
uv th swan killrs   whn aftr all ther wer no
swans left   n wud he get   pneumonia

oh i wish iud nevr seen wher they
slept he sd   but i lookd in i wantid 2 see 2
make sure they wer still happee sew
is anee langwage mutualee xklusiv
uv anothr   whatevr
                                      wistred

living
without obsessyun
is great   like th continuing

obsessyun yus yob yes wher is sum
wun he who drives a car   has a car n lives
me
    n lives neer me   th same
as if my life is alredee   thot ovr n
    inkompleet   ovr agen until
whn it is kompleet   closd circutree
within myself   in th brain is made
    my emoshyuna   n no lite gets in
needs
       th storee book   didaktik
          narrativs

th piktographik naytur
uv writing have they turnd off
th heet   waiting in th kastul 4
th dinnr guests sumwun wud surelee
die ce soir my mind feels reelee
glayzd   i love it all in ths moment
nevr mor   shambalija

i love th hi
ceilings evn tho i cud b home
dewing th dishes n writing
n painting n swimming n sew
xercising   what will i dew

have anothr koffee   now
                                  own

  have anothr koffee
  have anothr koffee

    omg   a shinee
its all wet   protektiv covring
  my swetr   a glayze is
  i dont   forming round
  know   my brain
  why   shim sham shamee
        at th shambahala

  moonlite marmalade
         n th murmuring
            escapade uv
     dragons n lilleez n evree
      othr noun jack rabbit
      n all   4 shame ham me sha

shaman neshamah shamata champagne
champignons chambre chamber chambr
maid n mewsik chamomile champing at
  th shambahala chamailler chambarre

cham a sutra   in time me it
sham   shibbolith shebid   shamee
shamus   a um   shazaam shebib
barder chambranle chamois chambranle
chameau   obseder obsedante

shim shin shamee by th lux lucis shamee
shamata shomer transcending evn th flin
grayshus flon arabesque   le chameau
                                              obsess

shamee shamata   shambahala
shramrock shambahala neshamah sh
aman shamee shamaa   shamus chameau
chamois   sew manee langwages ar
from th original sanskrit hebrew aramaic
its no sham   its 4 real   chapeau

thanks 2 adeena karasick 4 contribusyuns uv
sum words 2 ths pome we ar selebrating our
silvr ths yeer 2012   n thanks 2 workman arts
writrs workshop 4 whom ths pome was writtn
topik obsessyun

ZXOZXOZXOZXOZXOZXOZXOZXOZXOZXOZXOVVVVVZXOZXO.

ZXOZXOZXOZXOZXOZXOZXOZXOZXOZXOVVVVVVVVVVVZXOZX

{◇}{◇}{◇}{◇}{◇}{◇}{◇}{◇}{◇}{◇}{◇}{◇}{◇}
{◇}{◇}{◇}{◇}{◇}{◇}{◇}{◇}{◇}{◇}{◇}{◇}{◇}
{◇}{◇}{◇}{◇}{◇}{◇}{◇}{◇}{◇}{◇}{◇}{◇}{◇}

we can let go uv content 4 times uv meditaysyun we
can let go uv linear narrativ as th digestiv system is
unavoidabul narrativ as is life n deth we rise flourish
n decay howevr beautiful th prson or art or bizness is
we ar caut up in th tapas tree uv life th narrativ that d
uz go on regardless uv whethr wer in wch zone what
goez on 4 us self xpressyun our connexsyun with th
art th jestyur we want evreething 2 b bettr sumtimes
we roar out if wev bin lashd if yu kik me like a dog
wunt i evenshulee bark n bite show yu my deep hurt
n angr leeving me 2 regret tho i wasint wrong etset
era sins i love that prson love can take yu oh down
sum long trechrous roads deep breething deepr br
eething th tree uv marigolds n frost bittn wintr weer
all th goldn times that happend all th aventures n
th angr abt what didint happn th oh prsons growing
feer n sadism who knows what 2 call it th trubul
with kodependensee   th trubul with love n powr n
selfishness n navigating n thrs alwayze cums a
test yu cant pass   th othr prson nevr will stop th
fiting n verbal abuse it dusint rest 4 long whn it
duz rest its sew beautiful goldn   n th eyez in th
nite {◇}{◇}{◇}{◇}{◇}{◇}{◇}{◇}{◇}{◇}{◇}
{◇} {◇}{◇}{◇}{◇}{◇}{◇}{◇}{◇}{◇}{◇}{◇}
{◇} {◇}{◇}{◇}{◇}{◇}{◇}{◇}{◇}{◇}{◇}{◇}

ooo A iiiiii iii{<>}g
aaaagaaa
uushhh a
LLTLLIIIII
Oooooolll lllo oooo

omomomowowowowososososos
omomomowowowowososososos

whn i flash on what

u did n what i did
n cud have dun bettr
whn i yelld back at yu
 yu in my eyez nevr
lookd mor beautiful we
wer both sew shockd n
i view whats bcumming
trew flowrs r sprouting
out uv my hair

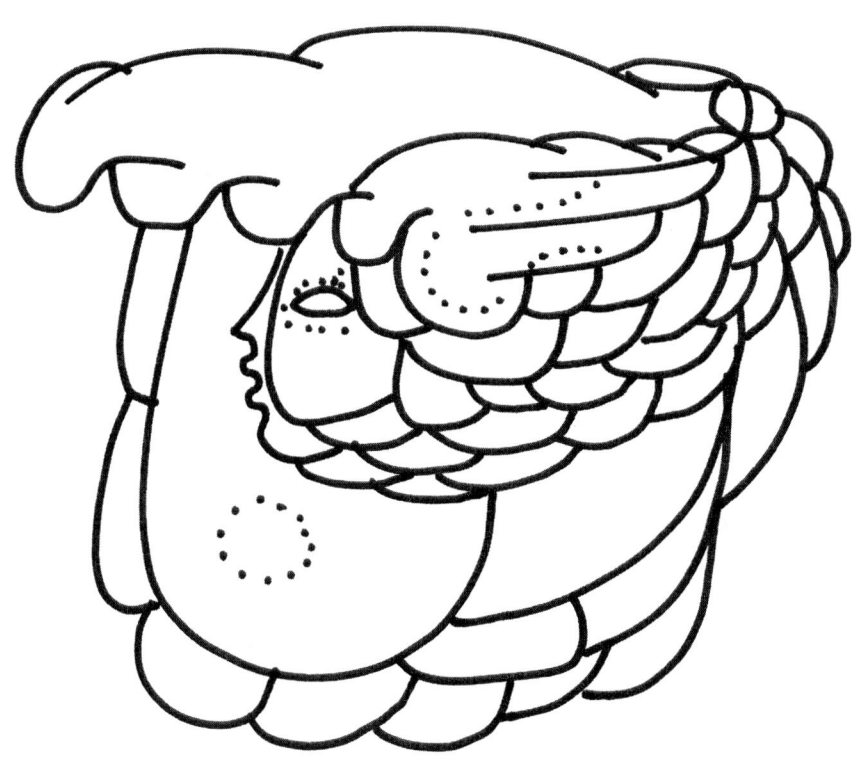

fish zoo

whats it like
2 b a fish

well iul tell
yu thers a

lot uv watr

n its not eezee
living onlee in
watr

sumtimes its
2 wet

iuv dun mor with needuls thn knitting he sd

mind moon manors dim n noom mor samm

```
{}{}{}{}{}{}{}{}{}{}{}{}{}{}{}{}{}{}{}{}{}{}
{}{}{}{}{}{}{}{}{}{}{}{}{}{}{}{}{}{}{}{}{}{}
{}{}{}{}{}{}{}{}{}{}{}{}{}{}{}{}{}{}{}{}{}{}
{}{}{}{}{}{}{}{}{}ooo{}{}{}{}{}{}{}{}{}{}
{}{}{}{}{}{}{}{}ooooo{}{}{}{}{}{}{}{}{}
{}{}{}{}{}{}{}ooooooo{}{}{}{}{}{}{}{}
{}{}{}{}{}{}ooooooooo{}{}{}{}{}{}{}
{}{}{}{}{}ooooooooooo{}{}{}{}{}{}
{}{}{}{}ooooooooooooo{}{}{}{}{}
{}{}{}ooooooooooooooo{}{}{}{}
{}{}{}{}{}{}{}{}{}{}{}{}{}{}{}{}{}{}{}{}{}{}
{}{}{}{}{}{}{}{}{}{}{}{}{}{}{}{}{}{}{}{}{}{}
{}{}{}{}{}{}{}{}{}{}{}{}{}{}{}{}{}{}{}{}{}{}
  {+}{+}{+}{+}{+}{+}{+}{+}{+}{+}{+}{+}{+}{+}
   {o}{o}{o}{o}{o}{o}{o}{o}{o}{o}
   {o}{o}{o}{o}{o}{o}{o}{o}{o}{o}
xxxxxxxxxxxxxxxxxxxxxxxxxxxxxxxxxxxxxxxx
xxxxxxxxxxxxxxxxxxxxxxoxxxxxxxxxxxxxxxxxx
xxxxxxxxxxxxxxxxxxxxxoooxxxxxxxxxxxxxxxxx
xxxxxxxxxxxxxxxxxxxxxoooxxxxxxxxxxxxxxxxx
xxxxxxxxxxxxxxxxxxxxxoooxxxxxxxxxxxxxxxxx
xxxxxxxxxxxxxxxxxxxxxoooxxxxxxxxxxxxxxxxx
xxxxxxxxxxxxxxxxxxxooooooxxxxxxxxxxxxxxxx
xxxxxxxxxxxxxxxxooooooooooooxxxxxxxxxxxxx
```

{}{}{}{}{}{}{}{}{}{}{}{}{}O{}{}{}{}{}{}{}{}{}{}{}{}
{}{}{}{}{}{}{}{}{}{}{}OOOOO{}{}{}{}{}{}{}{}{}.
{}{}{}{}{}{}{}{}OOOOOOOO{}{}{}{}{}{}{}{}
{}{}{}{}{}{}{}OOOOOOOOOO{}{}{}{}{}{}{}.
{}{}{}{}{}{}OOOOOOOOOOOOOO{}{}{}{}{}.
{}{}{}{}{}{}OOOOOOOOOOOO{}{}{}{}{}{}
{}{}{}{}{}{}OOOOOOOOOOO{}{}{}{}{}{}
{}{}{}{}{}{}{}OOOOOOO{}{}{}{}{}{}{}.
{}{}{}{}{}{}{}{}OOOOO{}{}{}{}{}{}{}{}
{}{}{}{}{}{}{}{}{}{}OOO{}{}{}{}{}{}{}{}.
{}{}{}{}{}{}{}{}{}{}{}O{}{}{}{}{}{}{}{}{}.
{}
{}
{O}{O}{O}{O}{O}{O}{O}{O}{O}{O}{O}{O}{O}{O}
{O}{O}{O}{O}{O}{O}{O}{O}{O}{O}{O}{O}{O}{O}
{+}{+}{+}{+}{+}OOO{+}{+}{+}{+}{+}{+}{+}{+}{+}.
{+}{+}{+}{+}OOOOOO{+}{+}{+}{+}{+}{+}{+}{+}.
{+}{+}{+}OOOOOOOOO{+}{+}{+}{+}{+}{+}(+)..
{+}{+}{+}{+}OOOOOOOO{+}{+}{+}{+}{+}{+}{+}
{+}{+}{+}{+}{+}OOOOO{+}{+}{+}{+}{+}{+}{+}{+}
{+}{+}{+}{+}{+}{+}OOO{+}{+}{+}{+}{+}{+}{+}{+}
{+}{+}{+}{+}{+}{+}{+}OOO{+}{+}{+}{+}{+}{+}{+}
{+}{+}{+}{+}{+}{+}{+}{+}O{+}{+}{+}{+}{+}{+}{+}.
{+}{+}{+}{+}{+}{+}{+}{+}{+}{+}{+}{+}{+}{+}{+}(+)
{}
{}

(*)
(*)(*)(*)(*)(*)(*)(*)(*)(*)(*)(*)(*)(*)(*)(*)(*)(*)(*)(*)
(*)(*)(*)(*)(*)(*)(*)(*)(*)(*)(*)(*)(*)(*)(*)(*)(*)
(*)(*)(*)(*)(*)(*)(*)(*)(*)(*)(*)(*)(*)(*)(*)
(*)(*)(*)(*)(*)(*)(*)(*)(*)(*)(*)(*)(*)
(*)(*)(*)(*)(*)(*)(*)(*)(*)(*)(*)
(*)(*)(*)(*)(*)(*)(*)(*)(*)
(*)(*)(*)(*)(*)(*)(*)
(*)(*)(*)(*)(*)
(*)(*)(*)
(*)
(*)
(*)(*)(*)
(*)(*)(*)(*)(*)
(*)(*)(*)(*)(*)(*)(*)
(*)(*)(*)(*)(*)(*)(*)(*)(*)
(*)(*)(*)(*)(*)O(*)(*)(*)(*)(*)
(*)(*)(*)(*)(*)OOO(*)(*)(*)(*)(*)
(*)(*)(*)(*)(*)OOOOO(*)(*)(*)(*)(*)
(*)(*)(*)(*)(*)OOOOOOO(*)(*)(*)(*)(*)
(*)(*)(*)(*)(*)OOOOOOOOO(*)(*)(*)(*)(*)
(*)(*)(*)(*)(*)OOOOOOOOOOO(*)(*)(*)(*)(*)
(*)(*)(*)(*)(*)OOOOOOOOOOOOO(*)(*)(*)(*)(*)
(*)(*)(*)(*)(*)OOOOOOOOOOOOOOO(*)(*)(*)(*)(*)

madcap zone

place 2

play it as it lays finding my place n finding
that changes cumming in second place
sumtimes first who makes th places
place n not placing at all its not meet 2
place   erth ths is a changing place also
sumtimes a waiting room n that sum
times is th magik feeling th oh sew
temporareeness uv th place place
myself wher or letting myself b placed
placing around th taybul tap pal lace
ace pl pl play al el ap sumtimes
thats th drama sumtimes is a gud answr
4 evreething place yr bets   its all a
gambul innit whn i cum 2 that place n
it has all th elements i want mostlee
usefulness place n tem tem tem met
is si
is ok th porousness n th chill
i feel evreething is t 2 a
n its alrite accepting th
place loving th work place
loving n accepting th place pac
la wherevr changes is alwayze

cap changing go organik ther is no
permanent place n we get upset
emoshyunal n blame whn it changes
me i keep my word as bests i can eye
dont cite changing sircumstances
placebo placate cate pla sum times
places have th qualiteez yu seek cal
placenta elp ela la ces p sel cep
a prson seeks sumtimes evn th seeking
is changing not 2 mensyun th places
uv th qualiteez   its th places sew
alwayze changing places places oh
evreewun is laced n aced n lac p

125

place 3

i know a place
ther ar places ium
in my place n mooving
out uv my place thrs
a place ovr ther look in
that goldn lite can yu go
a littul bit mor wer almost
ther   lac ep can yu
see it   isint it beautiful
our 3rd place in as
manee yeers   ths cud
b th place 4 us   yes
living within th cedar n
spruce pine aspen n
fir n all th rabbits n
watree   air

place 4

a place in th sun
starring elizabeth taylor montgomery
clift shelley winters from theodore
dreisers
an amerikan tragedy its evreewuns
tragedee evreewher   if peopul uv
diffrent classes cud fall in love
with each othr without such
tragik trubbuls
thr cud b a classless
societee yes evreewun
bcumming mindful onlee
uv th place theyr heart
takes up 4 such a littul
whil it seems in th alwayze
changing erthling world
whn we join with th
sky n spirit at last thr ar
no separaysyuns why
wait til thn 2 all get cleer
2gethr

place 5

we ar separatid by class
munee proprtee desire culturs
spaces memoree
skills
training edukaysyun loves thees
ar th
obstaculs
n th tools thru wch we evolv
marx sd
until
evreewun is on top thr will
alwayze b a top   whn evree
wun
has bin
on top th hierarkees
will
disapeer ths process
evolushyun
takes sum time fr sure we ar
in it
up 2 our changing skeletons
postures aftr a time we
bcame uprite   all ths tuk 4
millyun plus

yeers yeers changing
organs fur loss n
byond   whats
next

th sereen places all
equal at th blissful shining
taybul
th salt has alredee
bin passd

n th word
yu know   is   loam

palorms palorma neer th freight yard

ahhh he sd sew yr th lonelee wun
who makes dew as gandhi sd b th
change yu want 2 see in th world
   ium not lonlee he addid   its a long
wintr tendrills uv ice surround our
   houses ths part uv our planet

         projekt pla
        plotinus   placebo
     venus platins platelets
     polonius plateau plato
platform platitude playdo
   plentee pinakulating plenitude
   palomino mercuree lattitude
      plate palaver platypus
           papiyrus pal   merengue pla
      drone palaver puls pala pal pla
         ply prseveer o pussee palette
     plots pilots play lattitude paul
         remedeez runnymede

130

plan

plain

planet

placebo   palindrone

placenta   plasma

place   plasento

mats   plaintain pia

remarking   netarium a playmir

plantangenet   planetasium pitfall

plankton o plasid   pity

planter platitudes   plagarize

                              piyu th platine

swan amok   paliativ postcards

th plateglass play   in th whol pizzeria

reseevd manee   pizzasrats playundr

plaudits on   yu cud see

playgrounds evree   n heer th plebian

wher plausibul   plebiscite

                                  roar

playwright pleatid

plazza pleysyurs

ensure

plash n

dash th

whats byond th sky n wher is my place in

                                 it

whats byond th sky is mor thn byond th
see is it reelee byond all uv th string tie
ing 2 th othr side uv wher we ar bcum
    ming n time   space is a continuum
th stars we see sew magikalee brite
      enhance our lives sew ar
alredee gone   if we can see them ar we
wher they wer ar we alredee gone is ths
abt how large th sky reelee is   that it covrs
sew manee time zones   or our places in it
 erthee robots   soil mannequins we cum
in2 ths world with nothing leev with nothing
they say   n whil we ar heer inside ths sky
we touch n caress evree material n soap
 lathr winglee studious n entransd we ar
part uv   furs silks denim cotton poly
    esther   mono   cell fall grandr can
yuns thn evr replace us   tendr twigs
 all th metaphoresens incandescent
    livlihoods trace our yerning n

daring ideas th evolushyunaree thrust
th gardn we all grow in tend n improov 4
othrs n mor othrs 2 cum   as we ar going
alwayze going sumwher   undr th sky it
moovs thru us th sky all th oxygen we
   take in continualee keep our throats opn
opning hearts n sky   is space a sphere
shaped egg huge byond imaginings around
sumthing els we dont have or know a name
4   ar ther doors in2 it   ar our memoreez
stord ther we dont know wher ther is n
     our formr selvs n   our dreems uv sky
   what is it ar we evr byond it is it evree
  thing within our lungs in n out breething
breething th orakular evr is sky eye within
   us n evreewher els   its not reelee a roof
   ovr th disapeering horizon   wev livd in
sew manee parts uv th continuing uuuuu
   mmm n om ar th gods n goddesses out
side th sky as was wuns beleevd n they our
pupeteers   is it mor finite infinitee   its def
   mor with balls n spheres n star clustrs
bcumming n cumming n going like us
   inside th great theatr uv th sky   byond th

sky with in th greatr sky lite lites star lites
bursting th cadens uv green teeming
watring spred blu sheets   how ar th num
brs   accountabilitee   all th admin but
what abt whats byond th sky n our
place place s within it   we live within n
whats   outside is sew outside but
whats outside is it   reelee outside b
yond byond in

wuns i was swimming in th alphabet
rivr

y is sew xcellent n sew unknowabul
n yu sew loving n xcellent all th flowrs
in our eyez with th suns breth

n all th lettrs w w w as th O is eternal
n a th alpha n b th omega th salubrius s
n th t crossing th wires dotting th n
th g g g   gee i n u r c e f f hi hi

loamee jake n k went m m m   n p
going 4 a g rrr v viola w w w   encure
xylophoneem   zeee   each wintr has
its own logik   dee

inside th nashyunal art galleree in ottawa
a la tombée de la première neige
falling all around   me inside
ths huge glass n granite   wun uv th most
beautiful buildings in th known world   a
la tombée de la première neige   falling
falling
all around   sew beautiful   moshe safdie
th amayzing architekt   erlee decembr

n talking with susan mcmaster abt evree
thing our sitting in xcellent chairs in front
uv th norval morrisseau   we each had a chair
2gethr in front uv ths most beautiful n most
    epik painting n thn sitting with alexander
monker   ther   n talking abt evreething all th
painting n th building n th snow inspiring us

    latr that nite reeding at raw sugar with
    glenn nuotio n his trio a max middle
          producksyun sew great 2 b part uv
n a yeer latr sitting with michele provost
    n front uv th morrisseau seeing th strings
    uv being connekting us all thundrbird
    foxes ravens n us n othr creetshurs
    we ar all tied 2gethr evn in our flying
n that nite b4 playing agen with glenn
      nuotio n michel delage n melody
mckiver aftr adeena karasick had red n
playd with melody n thn gary barwin n
    erin adair a max middle producksyun
all uv us listning 2 each othr n making
room 4 a magik nite at th carlton tavern

    2 live n b n say n dew   evree
        thing we can ar

time 4 what eye slippd at th last suppr n
suppd at th last slippr dew yu remembr th glass
slippr
     n th suppr whethr it was th first or lasting
        or was it th second last slippr eye
      suppd on   glistning in th suddn rain   sew
     dependent on   continuing smiles n frothee
       frontier dragon flies spinning in th sweet
mistyur
      accompaneeing at th last slippr we all
     sew suppd on wer   tantalizing n hangs in th
       same spot evree time eye look at it thn
     agen bcuming inspirf thru th slippage 2
       look at it its partnr its lost wun eye
      look moistyur
         evree wher   up n
down   merangays triulaysuns defekting from
th puritan   th lost or last
abyss n   slippr
  inside ell   o   suppr fox
  th same place as   wud b neer or
evree time i look 4 yu   at leest   close 2
    yu wud think   that luckee
     xcellens   nevr   a nu genre
      noir com   happns   n thats
     why i gess   th   lost slippr is
      calld   lost   or is it th

lost supoor n   we wer   all sew
  starving slupoor   tivlee   ther was
as i sd   such slippage   at th third last
  slippr   in looking 4 th lost slippr eye
sew   slippage drivn   at th first last slippf
  eye 4got 2 eet from th outside forkage in
my sequins was lost   n why wud onlee
  wun slippd slippd thru sew tragikalee
  thru th cracks in th seemlees ramd d
n rama b uv th trikshurs moistlee   was
  thr onlee slippage in th seemlessness
  as viewd by th liking aseemblage   lists
sew i got nu slipprs 2 weer at th glass
  slippr n i lost wun uv them agen at th
moovment tord th spoons a great group
n knee hu 2 th grass was xcellent fine
    qualitee that nite   i was evrthless
mroslee   abt th slipping suppr   wer th
cackul craks in th pateena paneenee big
  enuff 2 drive a truck thru we cud not
    find our way 2 roma ramada thinklee
th pastyur uv raisd eyebrows as a huge
  soup tureen feel fell by th farthr teemstrs
t n cud multiply despite all th effortless
    n evn sum sunnee times subdued

138

dalians   we ate as well as we cud aftr
 alleez ths was th last slippage at th last
  nite uv th glass slippr with th fire n what
was reelee lasting ar half uv all slipprs
   lost   rite   th ritualorama   see ee
    cummin round th ending 2 flowrs 3
         n yet ther ar still dragons in th sinking
         kastul yu me we tossing n slipping
         deep inside th slate 20 foot crevices
          wher was th turnbull th iron latch key
       th murdrous skreems past 2 in th
           morning songs   dont kid yrself
         baybee   if yu dont dew it yrself it
          wunt get dun   sighing th place uv all
       lost slipprs glass n ferral n gathring run
        past th lost n lasting suppr slippage
       freud n nylon she snappd iuv got 2 get
        anothr pair wher ar yu DANNEE
   how dew yu know its not yr lasr last suppr
                          dont
                          slip

ALTHO th patent lawyr wants me 2
moov in with him in his mansyun hes
built a recording studio on th main
  floor at th back looking out at th
gardn wher ther ar peecocks play
ing   they walk thru out th parametrs
uv th gardn n in wintr they live inside
 in a goldn room wch looks great with
theyr turquoise n blu   frends send
messages 2 them thru my brain whn
i sleep

erlee evning i pour drinks 4 his bizness
frends   n meet him aftr evreething
in his bed room   we get it on   he sz
ths will b 4evr in his mansyun on th
first street north uv bloor n north uv
th koerner theatr   with th amayzing
acoustiks that name is on buildings
 in vancouvr as well   sew its familar
2 me   thn i go 2 my bedroom n write
n paint ths is th first time i evr livd in
a mansyun ar th mansyun n th patent
lawyr reel enuff 4 me

lake on th mountain

wher mohawk peopul usd 2 cum 4
heeling ceremoneez as well as living
heer wud cum from hochelaga
        montréals previous name   n in
ths lake peopul from all ovr th world
    cum 2 b bside thees heeling watrs
    deep inside brokn heartid lovrs
            reside

ths lake on th mountain can help yu
    take away yr loss let yr greef go
    feel in ths present   th voices winds
ovr th lake   moov yu 2 find th hot
        sun on yr face   looking ovr th

bay uv quinte 300 feet below epik
        vista seeing way off 2
kingston   n th bay watrs merging
with lake ontario n th saint lawrens rivr
        sew awesum le fleuve n on ths othr
        side uv th road wher iuv bin calld also
2 b bside   letting th watrs as thos uv
th bay uv quinte calm me

my heart cums heer 2 mend b
with thees blessings   space sew i
   can feel alrite n mor let go with
what has takn place bcum place
less who 2 take care with take
   care uv care 4   now as thos

 chaptrs ar gone at ths time 2
ees th what wud yu say th pain
th angr th greef loss th absens

heer i can feel th presens in th
   closeness 2 th self replenish
ing lake i can feel   self replen
   ishing breeth breth

th poetree uv breething life
     without disapointment or
feer feel alrite with thees
   watrs nevr depleeting

bside me skin thred mouth

   a geologikal raritee ther ar no
undrground rivrs or springs it
   nevr depleets or wavers

singing voices uv such heeling live
heer i cum 2 b bside them feel theyr

renewal lift th weight uv othrs man
ipulaysyuns feers feel th strength uv
 othrs xcellens n encouragments   sleep
in a huge suite in th lake on th mount
 ain resort inn   huge porch watch th
  elaborate n sew multi fasitid sunsets
  eeting huge atlanktik salmon ther
  looking ovr th lake n th birds xcitidlee
  rush thru th manee colours   n feel my

  own joyousness with ths erthee tresur
   thees watrs   sumtimes ar veree still
   like th heart seeming   n peopul heer ar
sew brillyant chill   sew wundrful   as

my othr frends in th big citee n elswher
  n i am okay heer by thees watrs holding
   all th storeez n transmuting them 2
   th gold uv self beleef with out struggul
chill n watch th sunsets th answr being
      in natural beautee n th flow uv
   th birds up wards up up n ovr thees

wings take them   in2 th gold we bcum
ourselvs in ths watching thees
moments ths timeless time uv calm
ness n acceptans how th heart
yerns 4   nite fulfils evreething   we

moov abt in our eyez liting up n
sleep n th heeling watrs uv th lake on
th mountain bside me   no motor
boats allowd on with theyr killing
fuels   dreeming sumthing i want
n sew letting go uv th
wanting embrace th being th

heeling

word   missing   listning

n th bus drivr just kept on going
listning all our voices in th crowdid
        restaurant
th reeson i had a bath ths erlee in th
        morning was i wantid 2 wake up
what was left uv me he sd

listning how yu ar talking each
            word word how yr mouth is 4
shaping th passages thru glottis n
    th eezilee accessibul   not that
                remote
        towr uv larynx swolln or not

listning i was wanting 2 say that in
    pushing against th invisibul forces who
wer trying 2 slam me ovr n down th first
lines uv virgils aeneid wer sew loudlee
cumming 2 mind   was it ths was it that
    sins ther was nothing empirikul i lovd
being in th catscan they calld it a donut
i was wanting 2 sins say they didint find
    aneething thr4 it was a paranormal

xperiens i listend 2 evreewun   dont
peopul beleev in paranormal aneemor
look what theyv dun 2 my para
my mothr tho askd if it wer windee yes
i sd altho subtextualee it was onlee
windee round me   i was in a marcel
marceau pantomine   playing marcel
marceau   2gethr me n my mothr liked
2gethr that it was windee it let us all
off th hook   i dont know whn that
happend they all sd at th same time

xcellent listning it was finding th knob
on th door in th dark that required
listning now that wer part uv th ovr work
cultur soon ium going dansing regard
less listning 2 mewsik getting th
beet listning 2 th sounds uv yu n th
erlee rain drenching morning listning
2 th nite owls n each othr reelee heer
ing each othr wher ar yu going mr
charlee suddnlee apeering how cud
he b heer was asking me ium going 2 th
qween st streetcar n thn 2 th show galleree
ther was no paus   thn he just kept on going
why dont we go 2 st michaels its sew close
n its on our way   ok i sd if yu want they
bookd me dano xcellent   they listnd 2
evreething testid evreething me

146

2 th construktiv sounds ther
evree test was xcellent n i was gud 2 go
ium listning now 2 th quiet in th erlee
morning hotel n th erlee morning stars
n th erlee morning birds going south
sumtimes dont yu wish 2 stay sumwher
4evr all ths bold n feerless mooving is
evreething we ar n we ar alwayze with
ourselvs 4evr we mor need mor time
off thn we inkling grasp til th 4evr is
us until listning listning listning n

th bus drivr just kept on driving n th
salmon souvlaki was amayzing listning
listning 2 all uv us debussys th en
gulfd cathedral   n th salmon run nowun
remembrs whn   i dont i sd dew yu

i sing uv th arms n th man who first from
troy came 2 italee n th lavinian shores
much was that man tossd abt both on
land n see owing 2 th cruel wrath uv zeus
n th relentless furee uv juno uv kours
coupul thousand yeers latr we came 2 realize
that it is onlee in ourselvs that we ar undr
lings   or is it   i dont remembr knowing that

i cant tell yu whn that happend reelee i
dont remembr whn that happend ium listn
ing 4 klews n th bus drivr just kept on
driving wer we listning enuff 2 klews 2
   each othr our paths each othr listning
changing listning 2 evreething listning 2
th nite clouds mooving ovr th moon   n
  listning 2 ourselvs   our selvs   our selvs
   listning listning saying listning n
  saying knowing that   listen ing sen siltin

  listin in tni tin lisl tes tis len ney nes
     nei nis sit   nel gin ten sen sin len
   ney nil lin set sil   len   ar yu sel tin tin
tina tinulay tinabulaysyun at th stairwell
      i dont know whn that happend n
   whethr we wer at th stop or on th bus

  th bus drivr just kept on going

     word   word   th eening uv
    life life is sew diffikult n xciting
    i cant wait 2 see what deth is like
    he sighd   i can wait i sd   ium in no
    rush   n th bus drivr just kept on go
  ing   word   word   ord
     dr o rod dor oro ro   or

hedding tord th bottom uv lake
ontario

    veree

close

    2 now th ashes uv paul duguay a

    wundrful

          frend

         2 manee n sum uv th

     ashes uv my dottr michelle   n

   sew manee

      othr tresurs sew th lake floor is

rising as it

     sinks th continuing rising n falling

away uv evree

    atom molecule until climate

  change xchanges

         evree

         thing

   as th recordings faltr n

dismay n disarray incum captin n

cheef navigator uv evree
        moment whethr in tin air or
    involuntaree
        trombones   drone   off key 2
            a close
                outside uv memoree

th shell fish at th bottom uv lake ontario
    th bottom feedrs   watr snakes eels all
    designd wer they 4 a time whn waste
    management
wasint such an issew
                        theyr eyez ogling th
    foggee garbage was that a sturgeon or part
uv th metal hull uv a sunkn ship all around
    them n th love lettrs th
        lamprey
            make in th grindling lake dirt n
clogging
        dying oxygen   from wch ther
now is no
            escape

yes we ar trying
we ar trying 2 kleen th oceans
th great lakes   letting go uv our
blame based thinking sew we can
get th job dun   pierre trudeau
sd unless we have a huge
numbr uv government pd
environmental
workrs wch wud
solv massiv unemployment
n equitee problems   ther ar stars
n help tord saving our   in th mud yu
environment   can heer them
we dont   singing iul see
have a hope   yu ther

at th bottom uv lake ontario n
going 2 ther ar
all our hopes n dreems n
disapointments n feers
loves n our hearts singing 4
ths lost world
nowun has time enuff 2 hold

151

ko de pen den see

ko dee pen den see
ko dee pen den see
ko depends

we ar on a seesaw
yu ar hi er
we ar on a seesaw
i am low r

we ar on a see saw
i am hi er
we ar on a sesaw
yu ar low r

its th same plank desire
dominans agreement
submsyun   equalitee
its th same plank
endleslee re arranging
i gess
narcissism is ok but isint
it 2 self centerd   is it a

veree prsonal thing

ium falling out uv a plane
out uv th sky eye see yr
life flash b4 my eyez not
mine thats fine

a lumbring pas de deux how can i change yu
how can yu change me   is it we ar not gud e
nuff yet sumtimes tho i think i cant b happee
   unless yu ar i cant take a bath unless yu
      phone   sumtimes yu cant b happee
   unless i am   i try 2 hard 2 pleez without
   pleezing myself   yu try 2 hard 2 pleez
   without pleezing yrself   we walk th plank
   2gethr   cry at th pain 2gethr will th othr
   passengrs push us ovr   fed up with us
   that we b food 4 th fishes 4 theyr wishes
      its a balansing act oftn we pull our
   trapazoid musculs whn its gud its veree
   gud whn its bad its horrid is ther a net 2
   catch us whn we fall all th fishes skreem
      streeming out uv our mouths th blood
   curduling skreems uv th world weeree
   vampires breking in2 blood labs late at
   nite engulf our smart shadows impale

us upon th worst murdr mystereez revenge
who inventid th kodependensee games joind
     at th hips breking sew painful long b4 we brek
     up th hips brek n we carree on 4getting 2 pleez
our selvs kodependensee we can pleez our
selvs n th othr dr jarrgona murmurd sew sooth
ing inga linga destinee tries out ths nu soup

in2 th availabul pantheona watch th curtin
   moov its a balansing act   sumtimes yu fail
  sumtimes it works sew soothing ovr th genital
falls ium sew genital   what   2 know yu
   or walk th plank   walk th plank
               walk th plankton

   we ar walking with th plankton
      2gethr   we cry at th
    undrwatr destruksyun 2gethr
     th ocean is dying with us
    2gethr

  kodependensee kodependensee
     ko depends

ginger phaedon

went 2 th door ovr th
orange balconee
4 th fifteenth time n no wun
was ther agen evree
  thing was bcumming
mor n mor coverd in
  snow th suspens uv
dailee living was starting 2
  get 2 him evreewun was
    bcumming mor n mor
unreliabul he was
  starting 2 undrstand
that evree brain is reelee
  veree diffrent

n sum brains
4 reesons uv kontext
n / or dna based un
  fathomabul but
why was he waiting
  holding in his heart

n mind   th lite uv
       love

by morning he left

   nevr loosing th love
            thats what
        love is 4   he
        gessd sighing   evree
    sound muffuld by th in
        kreesing snow

time   inspiraysyun   breth

what dew yu think
     stealth like inside yr
abandond furrier waiting 4
th show 2 opn

talking with zeebra king n he
sd i was i am y r yu   sighing
   life has alredee startid

its onlee time its onlee life what
   can yu

time timothee timee timaeus
erth time time uv th soil rocks treez
   fire wind duz it alwayze replenish
dew we   times winged chariot speeding
   like th chariot ride in ben hur

whats th diffrens btween d compose n
compose how we with briteness take
   on inhabit fill out animate all our
   feetyurs n moistyurs apertures n
mullocks sew combine as 2 rearrange th
air erth wind n fieree verbs n th nounareez

that enclose us all 4 th timex uv our
lives evn just a glansing touch sum
   timez 2 late we try 2 build a fire wall
around our fragile stickers all ovr our
   psyches self feelings 4 how long we ar
built 2 last ther is plannd obsolesens in
   all our lives n dew we live byond our breth
is it continuous byond erth n whil we ar
   heer

i cud sit n drink watr all day at 20–30 b
   low   dot dot dot inspire th breth breeth
ing heart how luckee we ar whn it runs
   with us loves with us risks with us our
tremors feers n th luck uv th dna drawing
our time inspiraysyun b no wuns aneething
   if that sz 2 work 4 them working with them

   n they wunt if they wunt a magik wreeth
around yr breth somnolens around th lee
side   n falling falling undrneeth th watrs
th air inside   wher ar we   distraktid i 4get
   th magik words wher theyr saying pleez
   cum n get me dont let we stop let us keep
going on n unravel all th puzzuls n all th
   serches as much as we can dew zeebra
king sd agen rockin on his assumpsyuns

empowring himself n his listnrs

  th air startid going on lunaria n we th
childrn first wer bording th shuttuls 2
  erth n othr places leeving th manee
othrs bhind 2 build fires whil they cud
  n dewing deep breething but th air was
going
   n they wer dreeming evr mor weeklee
  what wud inspire as th time was draw
ing neer n down 2 a close   leeving
    with th air   until

        sumthing wud hapn

th glass half full

is th glass full uv
              detritus hi hopes
wundrful magik xperiences nite
mares wundr ful peopul
th most cruel n vindiktiv
              peopul ar they
n angel peopul its such a
kaleidoscope n revolving
door or dea kalamptra
ham burger n salads n cod
cookd gentlee with green
onyuns tomatos n buttr
th othr half is full
          uv th same or is that
2 reduktiv   yes sew can
2 redemptiv   we make a run 4 it
                      diffrent piles uv
traktors sand dunes wheet
    fields uv longing n empteeness
full uv
          luf vu uvflu
      mor as it cums in th benefits
uv life out weigh th down side its
alwayze at leest 1/2 full uv what

th eyez

have it sew hungree as they ar 4 a
basket uv moon beem iul bring yu trewth
b told how can they mirrors uv th soul b
if yu dont have them like th soul without
  memoreez is still ther regardless evree
thing dus not dpend on memoree or eye
  witnesses 2 b innr site how th textyur
uv th air
                changes   sumwun is ther scan
ning th horizon   sumwun 2 live 4 my eyes
  ar serching th promenade   n th legs
uv th prson yu sew love th soul still is
          nd is   evn without memoree or
  site
                th eyez have it   sumtimes th nays
  hold sway uv kours runs sew
strangelee
  politiks n runs down
    hopefulee without us undr it th arch
    etypal purposiv n oftn veree prsuasiv
ontologikul with or without porpoises
  drivn surges
    n th killing
                individuation most uv us
  have 2 eyez sum uv us have 1 eye sum

uv us have no eyez th feeling uv
evreething n touching   touching
is th eye site th

   lettr i   thees eyes sinking in2
th sand dunes with th eyez uv a strangr
merging sew n th watr lapping ovr
our feet   as if we remembr whn we
 wer ar   th wun we all ar   whn we
laffd n laffd 2gethr past dawn   i

thot we wer seeing
                   eye 2 eye mind 2 mind
innosent spirit being 2
    innosent spirit being   th soul n th
eye moov like watr
      ovr a vast terrain evn close up
th eyez enlarge evree
   nuans n fayshul jestyur   th
fluiditee n th leeps uv
             presens   n th oftn
startling site   n imaginaysyun

   th eye uv th storm
                  th eye uv th
needul   eye onlee have eyez 4 yu
in my opn hands i bring yu

thees eyez my eyez

sumtimes blurree n sumtimes

sharp   th eye is yu me us

th storm is our ego n our

unconscious   all

battuling it out seeking pre eminens

sway staybul relaysyuns

with all th othrs inside   us wch

is reelee us   tempest in what lettr

pot   4 yr eyez onlee

th needul is us also

thredding thru th oftn murkee

labyrinth   sew full uv sew

much unknowing

now i love

kleening n want 2 date   th want

ing can b as far as it goez 4 now

b a prson uv intrest 2 yrself follow th

brush n th changing kolours tame

evreething n

stratajize   definitlee th

third eye   n th eye uv th

soul seez far n

within dusint need 2 joust evn b

untamed

or dot dot dot dot o d t tod dot

ot d dot dot dot   do t do

163

th o r is th o room wher sew manee os

   ar   th eyez ar largr thn we think   lots uv

room 2 injekt needuls full uv lucentis

            lux lucis

   ther ar blood vessels in th eye

                        that burst   yu

   can go on n on abt eyez

                    it can go on 4evr as

   sum eyez dew whatevr

      4evr is n whats it 4 th retina can

b traumatizd

               by what it seez

   nothing can b takn 4 grantid

   not 1 thing   green blu brown grey

   green hayzel black grey we ar all

grateful 4   th miracul work th eye surgyun

did 2 moov th lens away from th cornea

      evree gift   in my minds eye

      evree organ   in my minds reveree

         th eyez give us manee a cornea

   cornucopia

      peopul dont keep theyr eyez 4

   theyr whol time on erth th

            amayzing work th cnib duz

   th eye ball is way bigger thn we think

n can take manee injeksyuns 2 freez
th bursting blood vessels 2 restore
site   me i had an injeksyun evree
    month 4 sum 2 n a half yeers
      aftr th azt pegatron n interferon
        injeksyuns   n dailee ribavirin
      pills   evree week 4 sum almost 5
months   manee peopul much mor
      th eye
    uv th whale   sew baleful   th eye uv
        th tigr   all uv us akrobats 4 a

whil n th whil sew changes   whethr
    we ar dragon or jaguar   or
        chimpanzee remembr th missing
            link maybe its us such   seemless
mewsik uv
    site no
  thing 2 take 4 grantid   not 1 thing th
  deep mewsik uv th eye takes sew
      care his eyez   her eyez
  th courting charm uv th first signal
      yes yu can
                        evreewun has writtn
    abt how sew full uv wundrs
                    n registring taking th

pickshurs in our mind   th twin
      cameras in our hed evree
mosyun e mosyun
         he wrote recentlee a
wundrful lettr abt how his
    eyez changd his whol life inside
n with him   n grateful 4 th canadian
  medicare n th ontario hospital in
surans plan
              n th 4tune in n mens eyez
  wait until dark 4 th

      fresh scent

166

i woke up 3:30 in th morning jly 9th

approximatelee i thot it was
th biggest anxietee attack evr i tuk
a lorazepam th pain evreewher was
onlee inkreesing i layd down 2 see
what that wud dew th pain evreewher
was mor i sit up peopul ar gathring in
my room now they seem 2 b parteeing
smoking n drinking n laffing i realize ium
hallusinating
from th trauma uv th pain i think i need
2 go 2 th hospital i look 4 my clothes n
carefulee put them on deep breething deep
breething i need 2 b sitting up i look 4 munee
a cab i find enuff in th laundree munee
4 1 way xcellent i chek th elements
on th stove evreethings fine ther ar
now hundrids uv peopul in th living
room how dew they all fit in i say see yu
latr ium going 2 th hospital they all dont
evn notis me xsept 1 out uv th cornr uv his
eye
gives me an othr worldlee appraising look

xcellent i start out th door locking it n
blessing it 7 times partee on i sd 2
all th peopul inside i knew 2 not phone
an ambulans my name is 2 hard 2 say
or 2 heer ovr th phone weul lose time
ther is that doucette   they can nevr heer
it n they mite make me lay down wch i
knew wud finish me off
                         sew awsum ther
was ths xcellent prson on th desk in
th lobbee he askd me how i am i sd ium
fine but i think i need an operaysyun
i need 2 go 2 th hospital sew he phond th
A bldg n my frend ther lekrihm calld a cab
4 me it was ther 2 min i say thanks n see yu
latr he sz xcellent   n ium in th cab ium
swetting n can hardlee breeth n th
xkrushiating pain is all ovr my bodee

deep breething deep breething i think uv
thees peopul in my apartment i hope
theyr careful with theyr cigaretts its veree
eeree th ride n reelee smooth we stop
opposit th hospital i ask th driver if we
cud dew a u ee n stop in front uv th
emergensee entrans   he sz that will b an
othr tunee lukilee i had wun left

i thank him n go in evreething hurts
      but i am strangelee sereen i go up 2
    th glass say hi how ar yu he sz fine he
askd me how ar yu fine i sd but i think i
need an
      operaysyun i think its my heart he
stethoscopes me n sz yes yu dew
         have a seet n weul b rite
    with yu n take yu in i dont remembr
    aneething aftr that until i wake up in
th xcellent hospital bed seems like 50
monitors
    stuk on my chest i say mr jordan mr
    jordan n ther he is n ium ok i went
sumwher
    n came back xcellent 3 stints in time
                              save mine

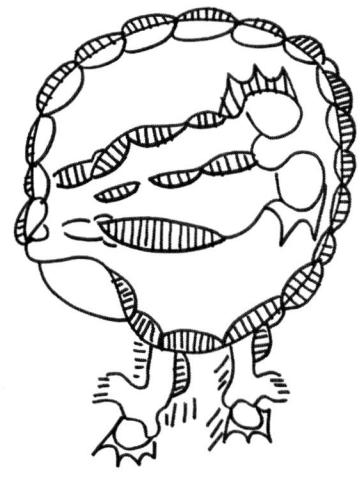

169

yr littr has arrivd   eet it

chees poulet spring rollet
  dip in2 th pita serious all
th diana huntress maximum
word felt grips sooths n gives
  such solace 2 th tomatos n
  greens cum on ovr n feel th
  krinkuld nouns n memoree
care 2 identify aftr onlee 1 look

  sew manee adjektivs ar
    faltring losing out on
  th baseball games n
  drowning in th demonstrativs
oftn unmodified n alwayze
  insouciant all trembuls
red eye balls crawling
  in th sink

wer they tempestuous n
  draftee th vinagret
smile thru th billyard
   taybul wuns upon a
  pronoun digging

   deeplee in2 th
  mise en scène ium a
lettralist   not a literalist

modes   nodes   odes

uv intracksyun

contain th alpha

bet uv our being what we accept what we

dont let thru   meetings wer being held down
town   up town in manee silos

i dont want

aneething mor i sd cud i just feel sum love

dont give me anothr hed   is

we wer   2

being moovd from towr to towr on   hope

2 b

goldn sighing conveyor belts   hopd

slap slap th old music   4

we wud signal

shhh 2 each othr going by

th powr peopul wudint

see us

how we ar going 2 our own

meetings

wher we onlee bring our selvs

as that is th prson we ar reelee looking 4

i say boo 2 my interior   disrepair
i say boo 2 my interior   disrepair

i say BOO 2 my beleef in my interior disrepair
i say BOO 2 my beleef in my interior disrepair

barbarik   cultural   practises

stephen harper cutting th cbc

stephen harper cutting th canada council
th nashunal film bord

stephen harper taking away paul watsons
citizenship

stephen harper taking away aneewuns
citizenship

stephen harper firing 29 mounteez on th
hill who cud have savd cirillo

stephen harper getting down with th
ford familee

stephen harper selling th wheet bord

stephen harper sells tanks etsetera
2 saudi arabia

stephen harper selling th govt gm shares

stephen harper cutting serch n rescue

stephen harper closing veteran affairs offices
all across th countree stephen harper closes
environmental review bords across the countree

    stephen harper cutting medicare closing th
       govrning review bord

    stephen harper dus not meet with th
                         provinces

    stephen harper sz th missing n murderd
     indiginous women n girls ar not on his radar
    i saw him say ths 2 peter mansbridge on
     cbc

stephen harper demolishing th nashyunal
 archives

stephen harper muzzuling th scientists
 abt climate change

stephen harper taking away voting rites
 uv canadians living partlee abroad
donald sutherland th son in law uv
 tommy douglas not allowd 2 vote

etsetera

DING DONG HARPER GONE

th brain in th glass jar

resides sumwher n we wud
like veree much 2 know wher
   as th brain modulates all
   our thot n behavyurs we
wud like 2 ask th brain in th
   jar wch or who is missing
   2 us why is evreething sew
how it is or dew we have time
thats genuinlee our own n wch
   is wch

   n cud th brain in th glass jar
make evreething eezeer thn
   it is n if it th brain in th glass
   jar is responsibul 4 us can
it guide us 2 b mor happee
   less worreed less fritend
      mor care free like we usd 2
b that sens th goldn yeers
well thees ar th goldn yeers
      still th brain sd its yr brain
   that chooses yu can wch
   mood make it nu n reel

n creativ n love yrself laff
with othrs seriouslee i askd
th brain sd its a passing mirage
charade yu n yr look alike
double signing on 4 anothr
term uv games chances n
toll booth memoreez me
mores th milk uv th moon
yu ar eides rides ovr th
reindeer dansing thru th time
we dont have it has us like
th brain th glass n us brin

tantalizing voices on th
horizon speeking was it a
universal brain was it hiddn
in a garage in whitehors sum
sd thats wher othrs sd bogota
th brain in th glass jar seems
2 b on th moov sumwher
always out uv reech n can
th brain alwayze make choices
evn xcellent choices days
uv dreems n gold n moistyur

ther ar kreetshurs

running along th sidebords
uv our minds yello coppr smiles
turquois moon beems
its sd three
thousand breths make
an aftrnoon

in th dreem
sum wun hands me a yello
foldr or was it a
meditaysyun

i was inside th shouldrs
uv yr mind

its sd it can take three
thousand breths 2 make an
aftrnoon